REMINISCENCES
ALL-AMERICAN LEAGUE IN ACTION

"We will select the kind of players that people will want to see in action. Then we will groom them, to make sure they are acceptable. It won't be like the bad old days of peep shows and Bloomer Girls.... The League will be good for you and your community, good for the country, good for the war effort and good for you."

—Philip K. Wrigley, pitching the
All-American League to potential backers

"We do not want our uniforms to stress sex, but they should be feminine, with emphasis on the clean American sports girl."

—Marie Keenan, League Secretary

"The All-American girl is a symbol of health, glamor, physical perfection, vim, vigor and a glowing personality ... the accent, of course, is on neatness and feminine appeal. That is true of appearances on the playing field, on the street or in leisure moments."

—From Mme. Helena Rubinstein's booklet,
*A Guide for All-American Girls: How to
Look Better, Feel Better, Be More Popular*

"...some of us could have used a little polish, but it was hard to walk in high heels with a book on your head when you had a charley horse. This we were required to do in the evenings, after we'd been busting our butts for ten hours on the field."

—Lavonne "Pepper" Paire, reacting to
"Charm School" as directed by
Mme. Rubenstein

"...they could be compared to the heavy-hitting New York Yankees of old. The majority are long-ball clouters. Their base running and fielding keep pace with their hitting."

—A Wrigley scout reporting on the style of
League hopefuls

"You had to see it to believe it, and even then you didn't."

—Anonymous

Girls of Summer

The Real Story of the All-American
Girls Professional Baseball League

LOIS BROWNE

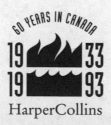

60 YEARS IN CANADA
19 33
19 93

HarperCollins

Cover photo: Rockford Peach Alice Pollitt is about to get her leg torn up in a slide. In the League's latter years, the leg burns became too much for a few of the players and some refused to slide. (Courtesy Time–Life)

A hardcover edition of this book was published by HarperCollins Publishers Ltd: 1992

First HarperPerennial edition: 1993

Canadian Cataloguing in Publication Data

Browne, Lois
    Girls of summer : the real story of the All-American Girls
    Professional Baseball League

1st HarperPerennial ed.
ISBN 0-00-637902-8

1. All-American Girls Baseball League — History.
I. Title.

GV875.A5B76 1992   796.357'082   C93-093185-8

93 94 95 96 97 98 99 ❖ CW 10 9 8 7 6 5 4 3 2 1

CONTENTS

Batter up! Hear that call!
The time has come for one and all
To play ball. For we're the members of the All-America League,
We come from cities near and far.
We've got Canadians, Irishmen and Swedes,
We're all for one, we're one for all,
We're All-American.
Each girl stands, her head so proudly high,
Her motto Do Or Die.
She's not the one to use or need an alibi.
Our chaperons are not too soft,
They're not too tough,
Our managers are on the ball.
We've got a president who really knows his stuff,
We're all for one, we're one for all,
We're All-Americans!

– Victory Song of the All-American Girls Baseball League
written by Lavonne "Pepper" Paire

ACKNOWLEDGMENTS

When I first heard about the All-American Girls Professional Baseball League, I was a researcher at CTV's public affairs program, *W5*. At my suggestion, the program covered a reunion that former League players were holding in Saskatchewan. Viewers loved it, and it was from my work as researcher on that piece that I had the chance to write this book. Since then, everyone I've spoken to about the League has been encouraging and interested in the book's progress. I would like to thank:

my friends and colleagues at CTV's *W5*, particularly Pam Bertrand, for the great job she did producing the segment on the All-American League reunion;

Stan and Nancy Colbert of HarperCollins Canada who saw the *W5* piece and liked it enough to suggest I write a book;

to the All-American Girls Professional Baseball League who made time for me, with special thanks to Arleene Johnson Noga in Regina, Fran Janssen in South Bend, Indiana, Dorothy Ferguson Key in Rockford, Illinois, Marilyn Jenkins and Earlene

"Beans" Risinger in Grand Rapids, Michigan and Helen Nicol Fox in Phoenix, Arizona; and to all the others who were helpful: Lou Arnold, Mary Baker, Arnold Bauer, Marge Callaghan, Faye Dancer, Judy Dusanko, Thelma "Tiby" Eisen, Madeline English, Merrie Fidler, Don Key, Harold Greiner, Dorothy Harrell Doyle, Irene Hickson, Dorothy Hunter, Lillian Jackson, Christine Jewett Beckett, Betsy Jochum, Daisy and Dave Junor, Dorothy Kamenshek, Sophie Kurys, Fred Leo, Mildred Lundahl, Elizabeth Mahon, Ruby Knezovich Martz, Lucille Moore, Carl Orwant, Lavonne "Pepper" Paire Davis, Janet Perkins, Mary Rountree, Doris Satterfield, Yolanda Schick, Dorothy Schroeder, Ken Sells, Mary Shastal, Twila Shively, Betty Tucker, Alice Udall (daughter of Bill Allington), Sue Waddell, Joanne Winter, Connie Wisniewski, Alma "Gabby" Ziegler and Jethro Kyle, curator of the Sports Research Department, University of Notre Dame, South Bend, Indiana;

and to my friends who encouraged me, with special thanks to Johanna Brand and Lin Gibson whose support and good advice were invaluable to me.

PREFACE

To tell the story of the All-American Girls Professional Baseball League is to illuminate an important part of sports and women's history.

Most of the women mentioned here are still alive, and most of them spoke to me of their memories as professional baseball players. However, as they constantly reminded me when I asked for some behind-the-scenes insights: "We were just kids then, and all we wanted to do was play baseball."

In the 1940s, they were, by and large, teenage girls employed by middle-aged and older men who wanted them to play the best baseball they could and otherwise keep out of trouble. How decisions were made and by whom, how the League was organized and managed, who made decisions concerning changes to the game were, by and large, questions beyond their knowledge. Moreover, it was not an era when women, especially very young women, were expected to share their opinions with their elders. Of the players under contract to the All-American Girls Professional Baseball League, former player Joanne Winter says: "We were chattel."

In the era of the All-American, every female—regardless of age—was a "girl," and almost all references in print or in interviews are to the "girls" of the AAGPBL. In truth, it defined very well their relationship to the parent-figures who had control of their lives. I gave up early on trying to fight the tide, and the language of the time is reflected here.

Among the players, even memories of specific games, or the championship battle in a specific year, have faded. What they all remember most clearly is the camaraderie.

For nearly thirty years after it folded in 1954, the League disappeared, except for the friendships that they did not allow to lapse. Any references you find in today's baseball encyclopedias—and they are not extensive—are due to awakened interest in the last decade.

In the 1980s, these women—now in their sixties and seventies—found each other again. They have formed a League Association of former players and hold regular reunions. The prospect of seeing best friends and teammates again each year has had an effect on the League's oral history. When they get together, these former professional ball players do what a lot of old ball players do—they tell stories, and some of them are just about as true as ball players' stories usually are.

Every player seems to have kept a scrapbook of newspaper coverage of her team's progress during the season, and issues that were important to the League, and to fanatic followers of the individual teams, were regularly reported in the press. One of the first tasks of the League Association was to set up an archive to hold players' personal records, scrapbooks and other memorabilia. The archive is located in South Bend, at the Northern Indiana Historical Society, and it's open to the public.

For the more businesslike details of the League's progress from birth to death, there are scattered records available. Minutes of the League board meetings and correspondence between club officials and the League head office still exist. Thanks to a rather cantankerous dentist in South Bend, Indiana—Dr. Harold Dailey—there are also fairly detailed records of the life of one of the clubs, the South Bend Blue Sox. They are housed at Notre Dame University in South Bend, Indiana.

Like anyone who has done any research on the League, I consulted Merrie Fidler, today a teacher in northern California. In the mid-1970s, Ms. Fidler researched and wrote a master's thesis on the League, providing a base for all subsequent research. She generously shared her material with me, including copies of taped interviews with Arthur Meyerhoff and others connected to the League who have since passed away.

Many people took the time to help me in my research by sharing their memories and their mementos.

INTRODUCTION

There were more than 550 players in the All-American League by the time it was all over. At least one was only fifteen years old when first recruited; most were in their late teens or early twenties. The oldest was twenty-eight, or so she said. The scout suggested that she knock off a couple of birthdays, just to improve her chances. Then again, maybe she already had.

They came from all over North America. Roughly 10 percent were Canadians, but half that number came from the province of Saskatchewan, including Mary "Bonnie" Baker, whose well-groomed style and dark good looks established her as the embodiment of the All-American virtues.

They were superb athletes. Dorothy "Kammie" Kamenshek, rated the best all-round player in the League, even got a solid offer of a contract from a men's professional baseball team. Pitcher Connie Wisniewski's win-loss record for a three-year period was 88-30, during which time she routinely swatted 240-foot home runs. Jean Faut racked up a lifetime 132 pitching victories (two of them perfect games) against 62 losses, with a 1.24 earned-run average. One year, she went 20-2, hit .296 and played third base when she wasn't on the mound. Joanne

Weaver hit .429 in 333 at-bats. Sophie Kurys stole 1,097 bases, 201 in the course of one freewheeling summer; the All-American changed its rules in an attempt to slow her down.

The men who founded the League wanted to be the sports czars of a new national game to rival men's baseball. Almost by accident, they discovered a niche for their new league in small-town America. Never satisfied with the new game's format, they changed the rules annually, sometimes in mid-season, edging the game from softball to baseball in painful and often bewildering installments. Many players met the challenge with ease. Dorothy Schroeder, the graceful fifteen-year-old shortstop from Sadorus, Illinois, was blessed with such ability that Connie Mack (or Charlie Grimm, or one of the two dozen other baseball legends quoted about the girl pro baseball players) was moved to declare: "If she was a man, I'd give $50,000 for her." Schroeder never made $50,000 in all her twelve seasons with the League. Nor did anybody else. They played for pennies, because they loved the game, and because it was the only game in town.

They grew to womanhood under the watchful eye of mostly male authority figures, their lives regimented at every turn. They suffered shocking injuries without complaint, and they played outrageous practical jokes to keep the blues at bay. Many were lesbians, in an era when single women couldn't admit to even a heterosexual identity. Some were married; one pitched until she was five months pregnant. Another's newborn daughter was sent a contract, effective sixteen years down the line.

The All-American victory song inspired camaraderie off the field. But its do-or-die theme also stimulated stiff competition among the teams. On the ball field, Daisy Junor says, they were "out for blood." Off the field, their managers tended not to know which way was up. Plucked from anonymous sandlot leagues, the All-American girls became pawns in a chewing gum mogul's social experiment. Their rough edges were smoothed by beauty school mavens; they were paraded like starlets to a sensation-hungry media. From 1943, when the world was at war, to 1954, when it had changed beyond recognition, in floodlit, small-city stadiums on a long-gone circuit through America's industrial heartland, they played—against all odds and expectations—some of the best baseball anyone's ever seen.

1943

⚔

THE AMAZING MIND OF
MR. P.K. WRIGLEY

In January 1943, Philip K. Wrigley was not a happy man. The previous year, his baseball team, the Chicago Cubs, had landed with a thud in the National League cellar, not for the first time. Back in the 1930s, Wrigley had asked a psychologist from the University of Illinois to determine why his players won the league pennant every third year, then fell apart during the World Series. The psychologist did his best but failed to come up with a helpful theory. Betrayed by science, Wrigley then paid $5,000 to a man who claimed to have the "evil eye" to put a hex on opposing teams, with the promise of a further $20,000 if his players went the distance. They didn't, and the warlock went away. Nor did Wrigley overlook more obvious solutions. He habitually employed between eight and thirteen coaches, changing his head coach every couple of months just to keep the organization on its toes. Nothing helped, but Wrigley was unapologetic. "I really don't see why people think I acted strangely," he said. "If the orthodox doesn't work, why shouldn't we try the unorthodox?"

Restless experimentation of every sort was Philip Wrigley's credo, and he could afford it. He had inherited the Cubs from his father, who started his gum business in 1891 with $32 in capital. In 1940, the company's after-tax profit exceeded $8 million.

Freed from financial unease, Philip Wrigley was able to indulge his whims. He kept a set of tools in his desk and delighted in repairing the watches of astounded visitors. He rode to work on a motorcycle and answered his own phone (but despaired of dialing it; his wife did that for him). He perfected a non-slip screwdriver and assigned the patent to loyal employees. In the depths of the Depression, he gave everyone who worked for him a 10 percent raise in an effort to jump-start the economy; then he guaranteed their jobs for thirty weeks a year, come what may. He kept several garages full of luxury automobiles, with which he constantly tinkered. General Motors adopted his ingenious modifications to a Cadillac's electrical system. When his technical staff was unable to devise a gum that would not stick to false teeth, he suggested that they formulate a material from which false teeth could be made that wouldn't stick to gum.

Wrigley was undeniably odd, but his business acumen was not in question. He had increased the family fortune by a series of shrewd and aggressive moves. He believed, as had his father, in the vital importance of advertising and oversaw all the company's campaigns. He launched new advertising campaigns claiming that chewing gum helped to reduce the thirst of workers in offices and on factory floors, battling monotony and nervous tension.

Wrigley was also notable as a patriot. He was enraged by the Japanese attack on Pearl Harbor and saddened by America's entry into World War II. His responses were decisive and swift. Even before war was declared, he had consigned his stockpile of aluminum, necessary for gum wrappers, to the government.

Within days of America's declaration, he had dismantled the firm's mammoth illuminated sign in Times Square, which consumed enough electricity to fire up a town of 20,000 people, and donated its materials to the war effort (thereby garnering more publicity than he could possibly have bought). He sponsored radio programs about the armed forces and war workers at home. One series of broadcasts urged enlistment in the Women's Army Auxiliary Corps; another lauded the United Service Organizations.

Wrigley's factories packaged combat rations, including free gum, wrapped discreetly in olive drab. When chicle, sugar and other raw materials became difficult to obtain, Wrigley sent his entire output of first-quality gum overseas and convinced civilians to chew an admittedly inferior brand called Orbit, in support of the troops. Wrigley's competitors laughed; they thought he was unhinged. The public, impressed by these and other actions, bore with him (and with the second-rate Orbit) while the conflict lasted, and would remain loyal to his products when it ended. For Wrigley, patriotism and business sense always marched hand-in-hand.

Meanwhile, however, Wrigley's worries as a baseball team owner went beyond the fact that the Cubs had turned in yet another less-than-champion season. The war had placed in doubt the very future of major-league baseball. The 1930s had seen attendance plummet, with 1933 marking an all-time low. Although high in 1940, the numbers had dropped again in 1941, despite spectacular performances, including Ted Williams's .400 batting average and Joe DiMaggio's hit streak of fifty-six consecutive games. They would drop again when 1942's gate receipts were tallied. Wrigley had deep pockets, but he had no wish to throw good money away, and the future looked bewilderingly dark.

Wrigley believed that the war would not soon be over, and that it would profoundly affect American society in ways that most people couldn't imagine. He had discussed a wide range of gloomy scenarios with his fellow major-league owners (for whose business sense and foresight he had little regard) and with fellow industrialists and manufacturers of every stripe. He also relied heavily on his correspondence with Ken Beirn, a manpower specialist attached to the Office of War Information. Beirn had briefed a meeting of major-league owners in late 1942, after which he wrote privately to Wrigley. Beirn said that the Bureau of Intelligence had been monitoring public opinion about the war and reporting these findings to President Roosevelt. It had confirmed that most people would wholeheartedly support the war effort if they were assured that it was necessary and that everyone would share the burden. But, Beirn said, as the fighting continued and a manpower shortage became increasingly apparent, public attitudes would change, and people would become more critical of those not making sacrifices for the war effort.

In Beirn's opinion—which Wrigley shared—the real crunch would come in 1943. "Millions are going to have to transfer from their non-essential occupations to war jobs," Beirn wrote, "added to the three or four million who will go into uniform. This summer, every baseball fan or potential baseball fan is going to be very conscious of the way their lives are affected by manpower needs, because of their own experience or that of a brother, sister, father or maybe even a mother who has had to change jobs, sometimes with a sacrifice in income." (Beirn's projections would prove conservative. Between 1940 and 1945, five million women entered the work force. By late 1943, the Parent-Teacher Association was asking mothers to think twice about taking full-time jobs, for their children's sakes.)

Having left Wrigley to speculate on the probable reaction of citizens who saw generously paid athletes swatting balls while their loved ones were dying on foreign shores, Beirn concluded by stressing that a happy ending was not just around the corner. "We have not really started winning the war," he said. "We have barely stopped running away."

Wrigley didn't much like Beirn's conclusions, but they made plenty of sense. Baseball was at risk, one way or the other. By the end of 1941, shortly before Pearl Harbor, the United States had instituted a draft. No one had suggested that professional baseball players should be exempt. Indeed, the major-league owners seized every opportunity to deny that players should receive preferential treatment; they did this so often that it looked as if they were hoping somebody would disagree with them. They did, however, argue that professional baseball shouldn't be closed down for the duration. Will Harridge, then president of the American League, optimistically announced that baseball was approaching "its finest opportunity for service to our country that the game ever had—the opportunity for providing a recreational outlet for millions of fans who will be working harder than ever to help achieve our common cause of victory." The United States Congress agreed, voting in favor of continuing baseball to boost morale, but reasserting that players could be drafted. In fact, a fair number of players had already enlisted or announced their intention of doing so. Others, who worked off-season in war-related industries, had decided they were more useful to the war effort on the job than in baseball and had declined to return to their teams.

Amid this climate, the Baseball Commissioner, the memorably named Judge Kenesaw Mountain Landis, had written to President Roosevelt pointing out the need for guidance. Roosevelt's reply suggests that he viewed both major- and minor-league ball as a wise investment. "I honestly feel that it would be best for the country to keep baseball going," he wrote. With America on a war footing, "there will be fewer people unemployed and everybody will work longer hours and harder than ever before. That means that they ought to have a chance for recreation and for taking their minds off their work. Here is another way of looking at it. If 300 teams use 5,000 or 6,000 players, these players are a definite recreational asset to at least 20,000,000 of their fellow citizens—and that in my judgment is thoroughly worthwhile." Roosevelt's only suggestion was that the leagues schedule more night games to accommodate the longer working hours of fans.

This gave a boost to the trend towards night games that some, including P.K. Wrigley, were resisting. The 1942 season had featured a grand total of seven games played under lights. Wrigley thought that the game lost some of its spirit if not played during the day, and he thought that night games were unfair to people who lived near the ballparks. As a result, Wrigley Field—the last holdout in the face of universal change—would not be permanently lighted until the 1980s.

There, for the moment, matters rested. But Wrigley was not relieved. He foresaw an inevitable decline in the quality of big-league play as more and more athletes joined the armed forces. War and baseball fished in the same stream. Both demanded the young and vigorous. Professional ball could become, within a few short seasons, the domain of rookies and has-beens, 4-Fs and forty-year-olds, as the best players were shipped overseas. Would the public pay to see these feeble contests? Wrigley didn't think so.

Already the clubs were cutting rosters, sending players back to the minor leagues, which were under the same pressures as the majors. Presidential assurances were all very well, but the President was a politician, too. Further sacrifices were no doubt in store. Gas rationing would severely limit recreational travel. Perhaps the teams would not be able to get from A to B. The schedule might be foreshortened, with an attendant loss in income. And what about underutilized stadiums? Wrigley Field, for example, stood empty half the time as a matter of course, when the Cubs were on the road. Casting around for something to fill it—something to have in the wings, ready to go if major-league play was curtailed or canceled outright— Wrigley came up with the idea of a women's professional softball league.

Yes, softball. This was Wrigley's initial concept. Although short-lived, it made sense, given that baseball's place as America's national game had been seriously challenged by softball during the Depression.

Despite the elaborate fiction that surrounds Abner Doubleday, American baseball almost certainly derived from an English game called "rounders" and was adapted for New-World use by Alexander Cartwright (who, having launched it, would emigrate to Hawaii, where for a time there were more players than in North America). One of the earliest teams to play a game recognizable as baseball was the New York Knickerbockers, circa 1850. They wore matching uniforms, which consisted of straw hats and webbed belts. By contrast, members of another early team, the Detroit Wolverines, wore different outfits, depending on their positions.

Early baseball was distinguished by rules that set it far apart from modern baseball. The ball was lighter and much smaller, producing games in which teams pounded out more than 100 runs. This led to a rule stating that the first team to score twenty-one would be declared the winner. At one point, nine balls constituted a walk. Three strikes made an out, but fouls didn't count. Catchers could elect to stand fifty feet behind home plate. There was no mound for the pitcher, who threw underhand. However, by the 1890s, the game had settled down to something like its present form, with an overhand pitch and a ball size and basepath length that would be familiar to us today.

As for softball, it was born on Thanksgiving Day, 1887, at Chicago's Farragut Boat Club, where a man named George W.

Hancock, brooding on inclement weather, proposed a game of indoor ball involving a rolled-up boxing glove and a sawed-off broom handle. By the following weekend, he had worked out a complete set of rules and included the recommendation that "masks and gloves are not essential, but it is a good idea for players to have their suits padded all around the knees." A very good idea, since many games were played on concrete, not wooden, floors!

From this modest beginning, softball (known also as Kitten Ball, Bush Ball, Army Ball, Playground Ball, Mush Ball, Indoor-Outdoor Ball and a host of other regional names) came into vogue. It spread quickly, including west and north up through Minnesota and into Manitoba, Canada. By the 1920s, Americans were starting to standardize the game and teams and leagues were organized all over the continent; active players numbered in the hundreds of thousands.

The game generally featured a smaller diamond, with different sizes for men and women, a larger ball (at one point, it measured sixteen inches around and must have been impossible to miss), ten players as opposed to baseball's nine, and, from the first, an underhand delivery. There were plenty of oddities to stimulate the imagination. In 1908, the lead-off hitter in each inning could decide whether subsequent runners would move clockwise or counterclockwise around the basepaths. Another rule stated that teams could choose to count either runs or points, a point being earned for every runner who got on base. It must have been something to behold!

Women claimed the right to play early on. College students at Vassar in 1866 were playing some form of ball, but it was kept quiet in order to avoid outraging the townspeople. Three years later, a "female baseball club" came out of hiding in Peterboro, New York. A newspaper reported the first game "ever played in public for gate money between feminine ball-tossers" at Springfield, Illinois, in 1875, and a loosely organized network of touring teams appears to have been established by the mid-1880s. In 1890, a visiting squad was arrested for playing on Sunday in Danville, Illinois, to two thousand Sabbath-breaking spectators. By the turn of the century, traveling teams of "Bloomer Girls" were fairly common.

A pitcher named Alta Weiss played on the men's semi-professional circuit shortly before World War I. From 1918 to 1935, Elizabeth Murphy played on men's clubs as a first baseman. A team known as the Philadelphia Bobbies barnstormed around the country in the 1920s and toured Japan in 1925. Their shortstop, Edith Houghton, signed on at age fourteen and later became the only woman to scout for a major-league men's team. In 1988, when the Baseball Hall of Fame in Cooperstown, New York, mounted its "Women in Baseball" exhibition, two of the surviving Bobbies—Nettie Spangler, then eighty-one, and Loretta "Sticks" Jester Lipski, a year younger—attended the ceremonies. Spangler, despite her age, made news by tap-dancing on the steps of the hall.

For the most part, however, early women's teams were viewed with suspicion. Many people believed that they were prostitutes or freaks. They tended to tour under names like "Slapsie Maxie's Curvaceous Cuties," "Barney Ross's Adorables" and the "Num-Num Pretzel Girls." By all reports, a fair number of these players were quite hard-bitten. They played men's teams, and some of them—usually the shortstop, in a fright wig and two days' worth of stubble, so everyone got the joke—were men in drag. One such transvestite was congratulated by his manager for "making as handsome a girl as any boy on the team." Johnny Rawlings, later a manager in the All-American League, was fond of spinning yarns about male big-leaguers of his acquaintance who had done time on this circuit.

The game was dominated by its sleazy promoters, the most notorious of whom was Harry Freeman, a "dangerous and suspicious character" who was charged in New Orleans with "inducing young girls to leave their homes and parents to join his troupe of baseball players."

These early days are clouded by the mists of legend. In 1931, a seventeen-year-old female pitcher named Jackie Mitchell signed with the Class-A Chattanooga Lookouts. This men's team made headlines by playing an exhibition game against the New York Yankees, with their female hurler facing Babe Ruth and Lou Gehrig. In the course of this contest, Mitchell struck out the legendary Yankees. The newspaper coverage leaves no doubt it was a publicity stunt, but it failed to amuse Commissioner Landis, who voided Mitchell's contract, stating grimly that "life in baseball is too strenuous for women." Indeed, to this day, a woman is barred by statute from signing with a major-league men's team, a rule instituted in 1952.

By the mid-1930s, however, women were taking an active part in softball from coast to coast. It, not baseball, had become the national pastime. Softball appealed to people for very sensible reasons. The 1930s were an era of cheap entertainment, and what better way to amuse yourself than to play a game, rather than pay to watch it? Almost anyone could join in. Softball wasn't nearly as strenuous as baseball for the average player. The distances between bases, and between pitcher and batter, were shorter and easier for those who were more or less fleet-footed but didn't have a lot of stamina. The larger, heavier ball and smaller, lighter bat meant that you could take your turn at the plate and retain a degree of self-respect. The ball didn't come at you as fast; it was easier for fielders to keep track of and catch. Games were shorter—a regulation seven innings—which made for a more relaxing evening out. If things moved quickly, you could even squeeze in a double-header.

The underhand pitch is a more natural, less stressful motion; sometimes the same person would pitch both games. None of this made for spine-tingling contests; games sometimes turned into marathon pitching duels. Low scores were the norm and big-inning, last-minute rallies a rarity. It was all very low-key and friendly, and women liked to play just as much as men, because they were just as good.

The result was an explosion in softball's popularity that is difficult to grasp today. In 1935, *Time* magazine estimated that the United States had more than 2 million amateur players on 60,000 organized teams. Fairmont, West Virginia, with a population of 25,000, had over 1,000 players on 56 teams. Wrigley's research turned up 9,000 teams—1,000 of them all-female—within a 100-mile radius of his second stadium in Los Angeles, home of his semi-professional baseball club, the Angels. Such teams might be simply sandlot friends, or largely informal groups that were sponsored by local businesses. Players, in return for some equipment, became moving billboards for the likes of Tom and Jerry's Auto Body. Enormous numbers of people played everywhere—on vacant lots, in gymnasiums during the wintertime and in the 8,000 parks, complete with softball diamond, constructed during the Depression as a national make-work project. Some of them had two or three diamonds; a softball field is small. Every U.S. city and town resounded to the crack of bat on ball from Memorial Day to Labor Day. This was the American experience, and it held true to a similar degree in Canadian cities and towns as well.

None of this escaped the notice of Philip Wrigley. He may not have perceived softball as an outright threat, but its popularity was impossible to overlook. Softball was outdrawing baseball in many cities. Centers including New York, Los Angeles, Phoenix, New Orleans and Detroit had developed well-organized leagues of talented female amateurs. Wrigley offered his Los Angeles ballpark free each year for the state championships in both men's and women's softball, with the gate going to charity. People packed the place.

Wrigley had also recognized the relatively untapped potential of women as baseball fans. Even before he inherited the Cubs, he had declared every Friday "Ladies' Day" at Wrigley Field. In 1930, over 30,000 women showed up, in response to a particularly vigorous promotion. This touched off a minor riot, there being only 38,000 seats. Wrigley was subsequently forced to distribute tickets in advance at locations scattered around the city, and later to adopt a mail-order system. His aim at this time was simply to attract female spectators; he thought they had a civilizing influence on unruly men. They broadened his audience and enforced the idea that baseball was wholesome family entertainment. This was also the thinking behind his policy of admitting children for half-price, which no other big-league owner thought worthwhile.

At any rate, Wrigley knew that there was something attractive—something marketable—about women playing ball. He wasn't sure what it was, but he knew that to delay was fatal. He risked being scooped by the competition in his own backyard. There were a tremendous number of women's softball teams, loosely organized into several leagues, in and around his home city of Chicago. In 1942, one such league, composed of just four teams, had drawn 250,000 fans. The Chicago clubs had considered forming a more cohesive body, but the idea had foundered on lack of seed money and the fact that each team was controlled by an individual owner-manager, none of whom could agree on what to do. Sooner or later, though, these people might come together in a professional women's league.

Wrigley could simply have taken his pick of several of these clubs, bought them out and fielded his own full-blown league the following week. But Wrigley was being cautious. The Chicago softball scene had a somewhat rakish reputation, and its promoters did not always inspire confidence. One of the owner-managers, a man named Rudy Sanders, was consulted by a Wrigley minion, but scored no points for showing up with "a chew [of tobacco] in his mouth that interfered to some degree with his diction."

Despite this inelegant habit, Sanders turned out to be a font of useful information. He said that he paid his players about $25 a week (a decent salary, considering that they could also hold down steady day jobs and incurred no travel expenses). He owned the team outright, supplied all its equipment and paid nominal rent for ballpark use. He took the gate receipts, on top of which he sold the team as an advertising vehicle and received a flat fee for publicity—as much as $3,000 per season if the players did well—from a sponsor firm. Sanders's net income in 1941 from one team was $5,000.

Wrigley digested these figures, but he had other, farther-reaching ideas. In mid-1942, Wrigley began to canvass his fellow major-league owners to see what they thought about the basic concept—highly organized, truly professional women's softball. They didn't think much; most dismissed it as yet another of his zany schemes. Only Branch Rickey, vice-president and general manager of the St. Louis Cardinals, showed any real interest. Like Wrigley, Rickey was a man of singular vision. He was almost solely responsible for introducing the major-leagues' farm-team system, replacing aimless hit-or-miss recruiting. He argued in favor of pooled scouting long before it became the norm. His wartime contingency plans included the importation of draft-proof Cubans and other aliens, a course he had pursued during World War I. A devout Methodist, he promised his mother that he would never see a Sunday game, and he never did. He also reputedly kept track of the sexual misadventures of his players. Much more could be said, but Rickey's justifiable fame rests on the fact that, in the face of almost total disapproval, he broke the color bar in professional baseball by signing Jackie Robinson to the Brooklyn Dodgers. He played almost no active part in the All-American League, but he did consent to stand as trustee, and his name alone carried weight.

Wrigley had a grudging admiration for Rickey, but little use for the rest of the owners, whom he considered to be nickel-grabbers and fools. In his estimation, they failed to run their ballparks well. For one thing, they plastered the fences with unsightly advertising—unlike Wrigley Field, whose walls were covered with ivy (a hit that lodged in it counted as a ground-rule double). Other owners scrimped on ushers and other staff, and (worse yet) refused to sell gum, on the excuse that, since it reduced thirst, it would harm their soft-drink concessions.

Wrigley had other, more fundamental differences of opinion with the owners. His pet bogey was the reserve clause. Introduced to men's professional baseball in 1879, it remained in place for almost one hundred years. Basically, it meant that a player, when signed by a given team, lost any element of control over his career. His services for subsequent seasons could be "reserved" in perpetuity by the signing club. It owned him outright, could force him to accept whatever salary offer it came up with and could trade or sell him against his will to another team. Wrigley found this concept odious, akin to serfdom. "I guess it is because I have a sort of old-fashioned idea that if a man likes his job he will give you his best," he said. "If he does not like it, no contract on earth can cause him to put forth his best efforts."

Wrigley had his legal department check out various alternatives, but, not surprisingly, he failed to interest the other owners in any sort of modification. Nor did he feel secure enough to dispense with the clause unilaterally when it came to the Cubs.

Wrigley had a vision of baseball. It was, he believed, above all else entertainment, and it had to sell itself on that basis. In his view, the virtual certainty that the New York Yankees would

win the American League pennant year after year had contributed to baseball's decline during the 1930s. People became
bored; teams weren't evenly matched. As a result, there were
too many lopsided games and foregone conclusions. To draw
the crowds, Wrigley felt that there had to be a season-long,
edge-of-the-seat excitement about every game. It was the only
way to keep the turnstiles clicking.

Now, he saw women's professional ball as a controlled
experiment. He wanted to start afresh, with female players as
guinea pigs. If his proposals didn't work, he'd lose relatively
little, by his standards. At best, however, a started-from-scratch
women's league would validate his theories, which could then
be applied to major-league operations—just as the women's
teams could be moved, when the time came, into major-league
parks. He would road-test his premise, like the out-of-town premiere of a Broadway play, and wait to see what happened.

But Wrigley was also a patriot, caught up in the middle of a
war. How could he guarantee government approval and public
acceptance for women's pro ball in wartime? His credibility was
high, but it would be unseemly to mount a league, given the
valuable resources it would require, simply with a view to lining
his pockets or filling an empty stadium. He took a look at the
map and was inspired by what he saw.

The need for increased military output meant that a
number of medium-sized cities, forming a wheel around the
hub of Chicago, were busily converting their industries to war
production. The factories in question were not small. They
were aviation manufacturers, heavy-equipment suppliers and
other firms that employed many thousands of workers, who
needed the entertainment his teams could provide. The cities
were large enough (from 50,000 to 175,000) to support a team
and close enough (all within 150 miles of each other) that
Wrigley could monitor the experiment—close enough also
that moving teams around to play out a schedule wasn't an

impossible task. Wrigley decided to focus his efforts on these locations. "This way," he confided in a memo, "we'll be doing a sincere, patriotic job, not merely selecting the eight biggest cities where we know we can make money." And where, truth be told, he'd met with precious little interest from his major-league peers.

So it was that in mid-1942, Wrigley began to assemble another sort of team. Ken Sells, a Chicago Cubs employee, was appointed president of the new, and as yet unnamed, women's league. Arthur Meyerhoff, whose public relations firm handled all Wrigley's corporate advertising, became heavily involved. Branch Rickey agreed to be named a trustee, as did Paul Harper, the Cubs' attorney. James Gallagher, the Cubs' general manager, and Jimmy Hamilton, their chief scout, were also on hand throughout these formative stages.

Quietly, Wrigley's representatives began to sound out local business leaders in a number of targeted cities. In essence, the idea was this. Each city could obtain a franchise if it showed good faith by raising $22,500 among a group of local support- ers. Wrigley preferred that a number of backers were involved in each center, each man contributing a modest sum. This would demonstrate broad-based community support and, not incidentally, pose no challenge to the central authority.

Wrigley would match these contributions out of his own pocket. The League, located in Chicago, would provide a total start-up package to what were essentially franchises. It would attend to all the publicity and furnish everything from umpires to uniforms and equipment. It would recruit, train and sign the players, then dole them out to each club according to their abilities, so that every team would start the season evenly matched. Players would sign a one-year contract with the League, not with a particular club. At season's end, each player would become a free agent to the extent that she could choose to remain or to sign with another league. If she chose to remain, she would be returned to a pool and reassigned all over again the following year.

Salaries ranged from a base of $55 weekly during the regular season; experienced players could negotiate for more, up to a (theoretical) maximum of $100. If a team made the play-offs, its members would receive a share of the gate. All the players' expenses would be paid to and from their homes and while on the road. They would be responsible for maintaining themselves in their home team cities, but the League would help to arrange suitable lodgings at modest cost.

How would the League make money? It wouldn't. That was the patriotic selling point of Wrigley's plan. The League began as a non-profit body, and remained non-profit while Wrigley was at the helm. During the first season, the League didn't take a penny of the gate; Wrigley underwrote the entire enterprise. Any profit was a club's—not to keep, for the backers' personal gain, but to fund worthy local projects. In 1944, to help cover costs, the League began to receive three cents on each admission, which ranged between seventy-four cents and a dollar, for the first 90,000 fans per franchise. At that time, the start-up fee per franchise was increased, but any shortfall continued to be Wrigley's responsibility.

Wrigley's approach to potential backers ran like this:

You are professional men, successful in your chosen fields. You don't know much about softball, but you know that it's popular. Your employees are interested in it. They play it; they like to watch it played. They should be encouraged in this; softball is wholesome entertainment. It is something we can all be proud of, particularly during wartime, now that everyone, including the President, feels that people everywhere need a break from their jobs.

You also know me and my company. You can be certain of my good intentions. I have made sacrifices in my business to help the war effort. They are a matter of public record. Now I am willing to spend my money, to take a financial risk, to enable you to join me in supporting that same cause. You are leaders of your communities; you too should adopt a patriotic stance, as part of your civic duty. This League will be our thank-you present to hard-working Americans.

Better yet, we are sensitive to your community standards. We will select the kind of players that people will want to see in action. Then we will groom them, to make sure they are acceptable. It won't be like the bad old days of peep shows and Bloomer Girls.

As for the League's organizational structure, you have nothing to fear. It is headed by well-known trustees. This is a familiar concept in every city. It ensures the success of hospitals and schools. It guarantees the utmost respectability. You can be assured that Branch Rickey and I will have nothing to do with anything fly-by-night or shoddy.

Most important, you yourselves run no risk. I will cover any deficit out of my own pocket. Any profits will return to your community. If you do your part, by promoting the League's activities, there will be profits to distribute. This will enhance your personal reputations. The League will be good for your community, good for the country, good for the war effort and good for you.

It was an offer that held considerable appeal to these small communities. The possibility that the teams, if they proved successful, would eventually become such a draw that they would be pulled out and parachuted into irregularly attended grandstands in Milwaukee, Chicago and Detroit was never mentioned.

Four cities responded to Wrigley's urgings by raising money for a franchise and picking a suitably resonant team name. They were South Bend, Indiana (the Blue Sox); Rockford, Illinois (the Peaches); and Racine and Kenosha, Wisconsin (the Belles and Comets). Each of the four was to become a mainstay of the League. Racine and Kenosha lasted until its fading years, while Rockford and South Bend stayed aboard until the bitter end.

In these formative months, Wrigley was busy refining his plans almost every other day. A Rules Committee had determined the mechanics of the game, which was still softball. But Wrigley and his advisers quickly concluded that softball pure and simple wouldn't do. It was too slow—a pitcher's game. It held a spectator's interest in a municipal park, but not in a larger stadium. To speed it up, the basepaths and pitching distance were enlarged to seventy and forty-three feet. The result was a field with measurements roughly halfway between a softball and a baseball diamond. The underhand pitch was retained, but the number of players was cut from ten to nine. They played a full nine innings instead of softball's seven; runners could lead off base while attempting to steal. The ball would measure twelve inches in circumference, slightly smaller than a regulation softball. In short, the result looked very much like baseball as played in its formative stages, back in the previous century.

Other directives flowed from Wrigley's office. He had very clear ideas about the kind of players he wanted. He insisted that they be feminine—not hard-boiled or mannish—with none of the "is-she-or-isn't-she-a-he" aura that surrounded earlier teams. The subtext here was, of course, lesbianism, a fear that was spoken of only in whispers.

The League's attempts to project a totally feminine image were sometimes faintly ridiculous. Most players had a long-standing nickname. However, on orders from the League, they

were never employed by the All-American's stadium announcers because they might be construed as "unladylike." Year after
year, every team member was fully and properly introduced
while everyone struggled to remember that "Thelma" was actually "Tiby," including Tiby herself, who hadn't answered to
Thelma since public school.

But a comely appearance alone was not enough. Wrigley
wanted quality players, the very best available. He believed
that a combination of femininity and expertise—they looked
like women and played like men!—would intrigue and excite
the fans. He wanted a cross between Ty Cobb and the girl
next door—to all appearances winsome, yet a terror on the
basepaths.

Later, when Arthur Meyerhoff assumed control of the
League, he would deny that any outstanding prospect had ever
been turned away because of her appearance. The organizers,
he said, would rather try to make a ball player beautiful than
turn a beauty into a ball player. When the sister of League
player Viola Thompson was named Mrs. America, Meyerhoff
rejected the idea of having her join a team for publicity pur-
poses—until he learned that she really knew how to play. The
sister, however, perhaps to safeguard her award-winning looks,
did not appear on an All-American roster.

Wrigley was a man of his time and place—a benevolent
despot. He noted with sincere approval that women had made
a smooth transition into war work; that they were every inch as
patriotic as men; that they were prepared to serve overseas in
arduous and dangerous circumstances. Whether he expected
that they would return to their "proper place" once the war was
over is impossible to say.

Certainly—despite freeing his players from the shackles of
the reserve clause—Wrigley saddled them from the outset with
all manner of laborious, literally girlish restrictions. To con-
vince the public of their respectability, he borrowed a figure

from college sports—the chaperon. Each team would be required to hire one, an older and supposedly more experienced woman who would travel with the players and enforce strict codes of conduct, dress and deportment. This would reassure parents, husbands and straight-laced landladies. The chaperons would be paid the same as a middle-salaried player and they would earn their money by acting as buffers between flighty post-pubescents, hard-living veterans of the softball wars and bemused male managers.

As for the bemused males, Wrigley set out to recruit as managers former major-league players, whose names were familiar to the majority of potential fans. With the decline of both major- and minor-league teams, coaching jobs had become scarce. Experienced managers could be hired for not much more than a top-ranked player. Their salaries started at $500 a month, but they could, if successful, augment this sum with performance bonuses. Ideally, they would be drawing cards on their own. Some were excellent teachers, remembered fondly by their charges.

The League's first four managers were Josh Billings, of the Kenosha Comets; Johnny Gottselig, of the Racine Belles; Bert Niehoff, of the South Bend Blue Sox; and Eddie Stumpf, of the Rockford Peaches. Three of these men had extensive experience in the big leagues, but only one—Gottselig, who'd never made it to the majors—had coached female players. He was the only one of the four who would last longer than two seasons or achieve any measure of success.

As the best managers began to be reabsorbed into the majors at war's end and the number of managers the League needed increased, some clubs had to settle for second-best. Some of these men were over-the-hill, dependent on drink, beset by personal problems, and should never have been put in charge of a baseball team. Past achievements in the ballpark were no guarantee of success. Jimmy Foxx—known variously as

"Double X" or "The Beast"—was a truly outstanding player in his day, hitting 58 home runs in 1932. Unfortunately, neither he nor such personalities as Bill "Raw Meat" Rodgers, so named because of his boasted fondness for raw hamburger, succeeded in bringing much glory to the All-American.

But success or failure was still in the future. From such unlikely material as he had to hand, given such unlikely ground rules as he had established, Philip Wrigley's goal was to forge a brave new League of female ball players. His time was short, and so the search for players began in earnest.

1943

×

THE HOYDENS MEET
HELENA RUBINSTEIN

Wrigley had dispatched his scouts to the World Softball Championships, held in Detroit in September 1942. The unknown author of the report handed to Wrigley displays considerable style in describing many of the League's first players. The New Orleans Jax had been the playoff favorites. "In their attack," said the scout, "they could be compared with the heavy-hitting New York Yankees of old. The majority are long-ball clouters. Their base running and fielding keep pace with their hitting. Flashing spikes and perfect hook slides are regular practice with them. They can bunt to perfection. All in all they possess remarkable baseball sense and are considered by many fans as the greatest girls' softball team in the game's history."

Despite this glowing recommendation, however, none of the Jax was signed by Wrigley's organization. *Time* magazine might have been referring to the Jax when it reported that, in recruiting for the League, scouts "turned down several outstanding players because they were either too uncouth, too hard-boiled or too masculine." *The Saturday Evening Post* described the New Orleans brigade: "Good, substantial girls like the sinewy Savona sisters and the strapping Miss Korgan. Give 'em a cud of tobacco and these female softball players would look just like their big-league brothers." This was not the image Wrigley had in mind. Nonetheless, Freda Savona, the captain, was supposedly offered a contract, but she refused; the Jax were about to lose their (male) coach to the draft, and she was slated to take his place. In any event, the Jax stayed intact. It didn't matter; a wealth of talent remained.

Close behind the New Orleans contingent were teams from Chicago, St. Louis, Detroit and Cleveland, as well as Canadian teams from Saskatchewan and Toronto. All displayed a hard-driving style, and many of their players made favorable impressions. Edythe Perlick of the Chicago Rockolas, who later joined the Racine Belles, "out-hit most of the right fielders in this district." Her teammate, Twila "Twi" Shively, who would be assigned to the Grand Rapids Chicks, was considered to be the championship's most outstanding defensive outfielder, covering her position with "long, easy strides." The pick of the "short fielders," a second shortstop position peculiar to softball, was the "diminutive speed-merchant," Shirley Jameson of the Garden City Brew Maids: "Fast as lightning on the bases or in the field, she has a great arm and is a good hitter. Opposing pitchers say she is one of the hardest hitters to pitch to, because of her size and the power in her bat. She is smart and plays heads-up ball at all times." Jameson went to the Kenosha Comets, and on retirement from active service became a scout for the All-American.

Charlotte Armstrong, a pitcher with the Phoenix Ramblers, was fast, with good control and a good hook: "Her delivery is also very deceptive. Although there is plenty of back swing in her normal windup, she has a habit of releasing the ball with no windup at all. To a batter at the plate, it seems that she just flicks her shoulder a trifle, flips her right hand, and the ball comes sailing over the plate." These skills earned Armstrong a place with the South Bend Blue Sox.

Ann "Toots" Harnett was already well known to the scouts, thanks to her third-base duties with Chicago's Rheingold Brew Maids. Sturdy, well-built and blessed with a strong, accurate arm, Harnett was "a free-swinging power-ball hitter who sends her drives whistling over the infielders' heads. She covers her position beautifully and has one of the best cross-diamond throws in softball." She was the first player to be signed by the All-American and was soon after sitting at a head-office desk, phoning prospects in remote corners of the continent and urging them not to commit themselves to their teams until they heard what the new League had to offer.

Canadian teams had taken part in the championships and in occasional U.S. exhibition games since 1933. The scouting reports noted with approval that the Canadian teams "show more of the girlish side of the picture when it comes to the style of their play. Their actions in throwing and batting do not have the tinge of masculine play like the United States girls. They do not go for boyish bobs and do not have the fire and fight of the average American team."

Nevertheless, only two Canadians caught the scout's eye. Olive Bend Little of the Moose Jaw Royals (later a mainstay of the Rockford Peaches) was a "fire-baller" and "one of the fastest pitchers in the game." Thelma Golden played with Toronto's Sunday Morning Class, a team organized by a church parish, who were then the Canadian champions. Golden was supposedly one of the hardest pitchers to bat against. To see her in the daytime, the scout reported, she was almost skinny and didn't seem to have much on the ball. Under the lights, however, "she seems even taller than she really is. She cups the softball in front of her and draws her arms close to her sides, leaning over at the same time. As she gets ready to release the ball, the batter has a vision of a giant spider unfolding on the mound. And out of those uncoiling long thin arms, the ball comes zooming over the plate."

Golden's performance must have lived up to this heated prose. She was recruited early in 1943 and assigned to the Peaches. Before the end of spring training, however, she packed her bags and returned to Canada. The explanations for her departure differ markedly. Rumor had it that she demanded special privileges, including, according to Bonnie Baker, a separate hotel room. But Gladys "Terrie" Davis, another Canadian who, with Baker and Olive Bend Little, could be counted on to project the requisite feminine grace under pressure, noted that Golden couldn't cope with power-sluggers: "They started hitting her into the lake."

Golden told Canadian sportswriters that she didn't like the League's grueling schedule. As a rule, Canadian teams tended to play less frequently—perhaps only two or three times a week. The League's season was, by comparison, action-packed, with games six nights a week and a double-header on either Saturday or Sunday.

Wrigley's scouts uncovered a wealth of talent at the Detroit championships, but they were confirming what they already knew or had heard about. Though softball in the United States and Canada was supposedly an amateur sport, in reality, it followed the Chicago model; it was highly commercialized, especially in large cities. Firms such as Dr. Pepper or the Bank of America in Los Angeles, Admiral Corporation in Chicago and every brewing company everywhere sponsored workplace teams. Many were all-female teams. Chrysler had sixty such clubs in the Detroit area alone. Companies offered people jobs based on their ball-playing skills—a variation on today's athletic scholarships. This was a tremendous inducement to compete, especially during the Depression, and was as much the norm in Canada as in the United States. Many firms recruited from distant parts in order to field a winning team. Players were offered higher salaries than their non-playing co-workers, along with time off for games, free meals, travel expenses and other perks. This practice continued even when jobs became more plentiful.

In 1939 in Toronto, a talented left-handed pitcher named Bea Hughey, then unemployed, had agreed to play for Toronto's Langley Lakesiders on the condition that they get her a job. When a team owned by Orange Crush came up with a job for her within a couple of days, she switched—to loud complaints from the Lakesiders, who refused to release her. The dispute went to arbitration, but the Lakesiders lost Hughey to Orange Crush.

Helen Nicol, of Edmonton, Alberta, was western Canada's foremost pitcher of the early 1940s and would win the All-American League's pitching championship in 1943 and 1944. Both she and Bonnie Baker, who lived in Regina, Saskatchewan, worked in Army and Navy department stores by day and played ball on a company-sponsored team a couple of times a week. For her efforts, Nicol received twice the normal rate of pay.

By February 1943, Wrigley's plans were well underway. Thanks to judicious use of the Cubs' scouting network, he had targeted players as far away as New York City and Memphis, Tennessee. On the Canadian prairies, the driving force was Johnny Gottselig, who had enjoyed a successful career as a defenseman with the Chicago Blackhawks hockey team during the 1920s and 1930s. He came from Regina, where he had played amateur baseball before injuring his pitching arm, and he coached women's teams in the off-season. By 1942, he was managing the Blackhawks' Kansas City farm team, but he still had useful contacts among sports figures in the prairie provinces. One of his friends, a Regina-based hockey scout named Hub Bishop, was the person responsible for signing Bonnie Baker, who in turn pointed out to him an extraordinary number of top-ranked western Canadian players. No one has ever figured out why half of the fifty-odd Canadians who would eventually play in the All-American came from Saskatchewan, but Baker's theory is as good as any: there was nothing else to do there "except play ball and chase grasshoppers."

At any rate, Wrigley went public with his plans for the League—known then as the All-American Girls Softball League—in February 1943. The press release was couched in predictably patriotic terms, with emphasis on the need to entertain war workers and bolster civic pride. It introduced the four cities and their teams, heaped praise on local backers and hinted at imminent expansion to centers both large and small. This was the first suggestion that the League might eventually include franchises in cities as large as Chicago and Detroit. Wrigley stressed that the presumably greater attendance in such locations would mean more money that could then be distributed to help carry the smaller cities. The League's nonprofit charter was unveiled to general applause. No one said anything about Wrigley's actual concern—that major-league ball might be headed down the tubes.

At this point, matters began to pick up steam. Word spread among players that something was happening in the midwest, and that it would be wise to get in line. Mary Baker, whose nickname "Bonnie" was given to her by a reporter smitten by her smile, first learned about the League in the Regina newspaper: "I was in the coffee shop I went to every morning before work, and I opened up the sports page and there was a picture of Mrs. Wrigley with Johnny Gottselig and a model with this uniform on. I read it and said to myself, 'Oh, God, it's happening. Now, am I going to be lucky enough to get in?'" That very afternoon, she got a call from Hub Bishop. "I was ecstatic," she says. "I knew I was on my way to what I'd dreamed of."

Dorothy "Dottie" Hunter, a tall, striking brunette who worked in a Winnipeg, Manitoba, department store and played ball during the summer months, heard about the League from her friend Olive Bend Little. Little called to say that a scout had arrived at the city's Marlborough Hotel. "It was on Good Friday, and I was entertaining some fellows who were over at Carberry [an armed forces base]. But Olive came flying out to my place in a taxi and said, 'Come on, get in here, you got to go down for an interview.' So I just left everybody and went down there, and before the day was over I'd signed a contract, even though I was twenty-seven years old. The scout told me he wasn't sure they'd take me at that age, that they were looking for younger girls. But they took me, so I went down to play."

By May 1943, newspapers in Toronto and Edmonton reported that the League's recruiting was "playing havoc with some Canadian teams." An Edmonton columnist suggested that the softball clubs "who make it possible for these girls to develop their latent talents" should be suitably compensated for players lured away by the All-American, much as amateur teams were reimbursed by the National Hockey League. In Chicago, two entire teams were wiped out by Wrigley's raiding. The Chicago owner-managers were incensed, and they publicly berated Wrigley for taking these players, some of whom held war-related day jobs, out of the work force.

Elsewhere, players were signed up by ones and twos. Mildred Deegan, a catcher, came from Brooklyn, New York. Irene "Choo Choo" Hickson, the alleged twenty-eight-year-old who wound up being called "Grandma" by the fans, came from North Carolina. Madeline "Maddy" English, third baseman in a Boston league that played indoors on a cement field with painted bases, was from Everett, Massachusetts. Ralph Wheeler, a Boston sportswriter and sometime scout for the Cubs, came to her home to offer her a tryout, having heard of her from male athletes at her high school. She made the League, along with two other Massachusetts players, Mary Pratt and Dorothy "Dottie" Green.

Were they eager to go when the All-American came knocking? You'd better believe they were. Younger players especially jumped at the chance to get paid for doing what they'd have done for free. Plus, they were dazzled by the sums involved. Most were making a pittance—perhaps $10 a week—in offices or factories. Store clerks made rather less. Dottie Hunter's father, a family man, was making $35 a week. The League's $55 entry-level salary was unheard of for young women. Besides, players would be on the road half the time, with those travelling and living expenses paid. They could bank money and plan on attending college to make something of themselves, or they could at least escape from the limited horizons of dead-end jobs and one-horse towns.

But there were obstacles. Many prospective players were still teenagers, and subject to the wishes of their families; even those in their twenties, holding down steady jobs, were often living at home with protective parents, people who had barely survived the Depression. To a Saskatchewan farm family, South Bend or Kenosha sounded like Sodom and Gomorrah. They were hopeful of a better life for their daughters, but this seemed a bit much.

While most parents had misgivings, however, few were adamantly against the idea. Convinced of Wrigley's bona fides, and having learned that chaperons would be thick on the ground, they usually relented. The players, of course, had their suitcases packed and were two steps out the door. Professional softball represented the opportunity of a lifetime. Amid a climate of wartime restraint, as North America battened down for rationing and sacrifice, this was a chance for adventure.

In a few cases, it wasn't parents but husbands who cried foul. Bonnie Baker's husband, Maury, was stationed overseas with the Royal Canadian Air Force when Bonnie was given her chance to play pro ball. She had good reason to believe that he would be less than thrilled at the prospect. They had been married for nearly five years. In 1942, she had had to pass up a chance to play in Montreal for a team sponsored by Ogilvie Oats because he insisted she stay home. This time, however, her mother-in-law encouraged her to go now and tell Maury later. This bold maneuver worked. When Baker became the South Bend Blue Sox catcher—and the League's most widely recognized star—Maury burst with pride. But he accepted her ball career on the understanding that Bonnie would call it quits when he came marching home.

The players reported for 1943 spring training—held for the first and only time at Wrigley Field itself—in a state of great anticipation. Only sixty players would survive, chosen to fill berths on the All-American's four founding teams. They traveled by train, with one or two delays en route. War work had priority; so did anyone in service uniform. Players scrambled for early-morning or late-night connections, clutching cardboard suitcases and other must-have gear, including, in one case, a portable gramophone. Some had never been on a train before.

To many of them, Chicago must have seemed like another planet. Lillian Jackson, recruited from Nashville, Tennessee, was thrilled to discover that she and the other hopefuls would use the same locker rooms and showers as the Cubs.

All the players had been told beforehand that there'd be myriad rules and regulations governing personal conduct. They had received the patented no-shame, no-blame pep talk, and knew that chaperons would monitor their every move. Unsuitable behavior was spelled out in their contracts, complete with the penalties—$10 for back-chatting umpires, $50 for appearing "unkempt" in public. The League was keen on comparing its standard document to an Actors' Equity agreement. This suggestion added a touch of show-biz panache. Smoking and drinking hard liquor in public were forbidden.

Every social engagement had to be cleared ahead of time with the chaperon. A curfew called for players to be tucked safely into bed two hours after the game—just time enough for a shower, change and a bite to eat. Even close friends and blood relatives were kept well away from the bench; a no-fraternization clause prohibited off-the-field contacts with rival club members. All this was understood—but the League uniform came as an unwelcome surprise. Unless the players had seen the photograph that caught Bonnie Baker's eye, they hadn't realized they'd be playing in skirts.

By the early 1940s, young women everywhere were wearing pants. Rosie the Riveter—the symbol of a woman's ability to do a man's work—went about her business in slacks or overalls. Shorts were customary for casual wear; jeans (known as dungarees) were big with teenagers. But the All-American wanted something entirely different.

Most female softball teams wore modified men's uniforms, but there were exceptions. Clubs from the southwestern states, notably the Arizona Ramblers, wore shorts. So did the Moose Jaw Royals, from wind-swept Saskatchewan—but in deference to the prairie climate they wore them with leotards, which made the players look like trapeze artists. The ultimate fashion statement was made by Toronto's Sunday Morning Class, as described in the 1942 scouting report: "Their entire uniform is white. On their heads they wear a small stocking cap about the size of a small plate. The fact that none of the girls have a boyish haircut makes the tiny cap appear even smaller than it really is. Instead of shirts they wear a tight-fitting long-sleeved sweater that makes them appear like a group of Hollywood sweater girls. Flowing out from the bottom of the sweater is a short full-pleated skirt that barely reaches their knees. The pleats are very small and as the players cavort about the field they give one the impression of a group of ballet dancers as their skirts flare out."

Dazzled by this image, the League opted for skirts. The final version was apparently designed by Mrs. Wrigley, with the aid of Ann Harnett and Otis Shepherd, the artist responsible for most of Wrigley's advertising billboards. The result was a belted tunic dress with short sleeves that buttoned up the front, but on the left side, leaving the chest free for a circular team logo. The dress came in four team colors: pastel shades of green, blue, yellow and peach. Only the Blue Sox and Peaches were fortunate enough to match color and name. The skirt was flared and unhemmed. Players were expected to hem it to suit their size, but no shorter than six inches above the knee. Underneath they wore elasticized shorts, an absolute necessity given their energetic style of play. They wore a small cap with a large peak and stockings rolled to reach just below the knee. It looked like a tennis outfit or, more precisely, a British field hockey uniform. The result, according to Marie Keenan, the League secretary, nicely fulfilled Wrigley's intentions: "We do not want our uniforms to stress sex, but they should be feminine, with emphasis on the clean American sports girl."

The sports girls, for their part, found the design ridiculous. Dorothy Hunter, playing first base for the Racine Belles, thought some of the players looked "like some old lady walking around with an old-fashioned dress ... I was tall enough that mine came right to my knees. Besides, I had heavy legs and I didn't want to show them off too much." Players stuck to the hem rule at first, but gradually shortened them how they pleased. Lucille Moore, the South Bend Blue Sox chaperon, remembers that a lot of people were rather shocked because some of the players showed a lot of thigh. "Each year," she said, "the hemlines went up and up."

The skirts raised eyebrows and created problems. Joanne Winter, who was assigned to the Racine Belles, found that they cramped her pitching style. The shoulders tended to bind and the skirt flared out, impeding her release. "It was great from the spectator viewpoint," she said. "From our standpoint, not many of us enjoyed it. If I'd had a brain and a seamstress, I would have changed it."

Perhaps the most serious difficulty—aside from chilblains inevitable when playing games in the midwest in early spring—was that the skirts made sliding an exercise in masochism. Most players carried terrible abrasions known as "strawberries"—large areas of raw, scraped skin that would scarcely heal before another slide tore them open again. At least one manager was so undone by the inevitable pain and suffering that he averted his eyes each time a player came careening into base.

Occasionally, the League would attempt to tinker with the uniform design, but the solutions were always worse. At one point, Marie Keenan wrote the manufacturer suggesting that the pitcher might be issued a skirt fitted with an elastic band that would hold it close to her legs, into which she could step like a pair of slacks. This tube-dress or stovepipe concept was never inaugurated.

Some aspects of the uniform had players in stitches. Winter and teammate Sophie Kurys remember their first glimpse of Thelma Walmsley in a catcher's uniform. Walmsley sported a high pompadour, a popular hairdo of the time. It was without question feminine, but when coupled with a catcher's mask, it was also absurd. On the pitcher's mound, Joanne Winter recalls, "I turned my back to the plate and then turned around. And there's Walmsley behind the plate, and I cracked up." Kurys looked at Winter and joined in. But soon she was charging the mound, yelling, "Cut it out, will'ya! Straighten up!" "The whole bunch of them were after me," says an unrepentant Winter, "but you know how it is when you get the giggles."

During the League's earliest days, the publicity mill was working overtime. The writer of a Muskegon *Chronicle* article celebrating Arleene Johnson, another player from small-town Saskatchewan, was baffled when told that she liked curling, an activity many Americans had never heard of. The writer felt compelled to explain the game's mysteries: "The sport where the players wear kilts and make with the brooms on an ice rink, pushing little black pots that vaguely resemble cuspidors. The game is a sort of a cross between shuffleboard, bowling, ice hockey and floor sweeping."

Press releases centered on domesticity at every turn. Ann Harnett was presented as "an accomplished coffee maker." Clara Schillace "enjoyed nothing better than to whip up a spaghetti dinner, work with her father in the Victory Garden and wash dishes with her pretty niece."

Shirley Jameson was distinguished by "roguish eyes that refuse to behave, a saucy, turned-up little Irish pug nose, and enough concentrated personality to lend oomph to a carload of Hollywood starlets, all wrapped up in a four-foot, eleven-inch chassis." A League questionnaire, distributed to every player, sought to elicit human-interest data by means of questions such as "Do you get many mash notes from the fans?"

Extracurricular interests were blown out of all proportion. If someone had taken flying lessons, she became an accomplished aviatrix. Anyone who'd posed for a department-store snapshot was described as a former model. Choo Choo Hickson, who had just once donned boxing gloves as part of a publicity stunt in Tennessee, was labelled "Chattanooga's Only Girl Pugilist." The pity is that Wrigley and Co. didn't highlight the players' real achievements. Lib Mahon had a university degree and taught school, as did Shirley Jameson, who had also won speed-skating awards nationwide. Oddly, even the players' wide-ranging athletic interests received relatively little attention. Schillace (in-between bouts of dish-washing) had competed in national track-and-field meets. Dorothy Ferguson was Manitoba's top-ranked speed-skater, and Betsy Jochum was the Amateur Softball Association's throwing champion. The League preferred to feature more "womanly" activities—housework or piano playing, pasting pictures into scrapbooks and writing letters home.

Perhaps the strangest aspect of the 1943 spring training was its "Charm School," actually a mandatory course in good grooming and ladylike behavior. No one remembers who first came up with this bright idea, but Arthur Meyerhoff was an avid supporter. His conversion took place while visiting the summer home of Patricia Stevens, who owned a well-known Chicago modeling studio. "We spent the day there and everyone was in swimming," he said. "I remember looking around and these were all girls from her school, and I said to myself, 'What a bunch of homely-looking mugs.' When they left for their rooms and got ready for dinner, out came the most beautiful group of girls you've ever seen." Thus inspired, Meyerhoff arranged for none other than Helena Rubinstein, whose chain of beauty salons had made her name synonymous with the feminine ideal, to coach the players in elegant deportment.

Players were issued loose-leaf binders in which to record "Notes of a Star To Be." The idea of farm girls and small-town rowdies being given lessons in how to walk, sit, apply make-up, put on coats and introduce themselves at social functions was public relations gold. The Charm School session was the obligatory lead paragraph in every subsequent magazine article. Some of the players were grateful—to a degree. Because Dorothy Kamenshek's family never ate out in restaurants, she "didn't know what all those forks were for," and was mildly interested to learn. Even the stylish Bonnie Baker, who could have conducted the seminars herself, was appreciative: "It was important, because everybody was watching you all the time. Much as I liked slacks and shorts, I was glad that we couldn't wear them, because people tend to get slovenly, especially with slacks, and I thought it was good discipline."

There were dissenting opinions. Lavonne "Pepper" Paire remarks darkly that "some of us could have used a little polish, but it was hard to walk in high heels with a book on your head when you had a charley horse. This we were required to do in the evenings, after we'd been busting our butts for ten hours on the field." Besides, as Choo Choo Hickson admits, a fair number of players "didn't look any better with make-up on." Thrown suddenly into the limelight, meeting prominent people for the first time, having to cope with the attentions of the press, they needed help.

So the cosmetics industry triumphed, to the delight of newspapers everywhere. Aside from stiff and unconvincing "action poses," the typical All-American photo showed players lined up in the dressing room, anxiously fluffing their hair before taking the field. Another much-repeated shot captured Ruth "Tex" Lessing, an attractive blonde who played catcher for the Grand Rapids Chicks, with her mask tilted back to reveal a carefully coiffed head, a powder puff in one hand and mirror in the other.

Catchers did not want for coverage. Bonnie Baker was front and center in South Bend's advertisements, minus both unbecoming chest protector and the face-mask, which would have obscured her dark good looks. Some of Baker's teammates recall that she managed to garner more than her share of coverage, at the expense of other players, which Baker acknowledges: "Libby Mahon would go out and make four spectacular catches and maybe get three hits. In the same game, I'd run after four pop flies. But I got the headlines. Of course, if I dropped a ball and someone else hit a home run, I got the write-up for that, too, for four days in a row." Stardom had its price.

The Charm School was discontinued after a couple of seasons, even though a beauty kit, complete with full instructions, was issued for many years. But its message lingered on, in the form of a ten-page booklet, penned by Mme. Rubinstein's staff, with the imperative title "A Guide for All-American Girls: How To Look Better, Feel Better, Be More Popular." Copy read thus: "The All-American girl is a symbol of health, glamor, physical perfection, vim, vigor and a glowing personality. Being included on the All-American roster is indeed a privilege to be granted only to those who are especially chosen for looks, deportment and feminine charm, in addition to natural athletic ability. The accent, of course, is on neatness and feminine appeal. That is true of appearances on the playing field, on the street or in leisure moments. Avoid noisy, rough and raucous talk and actions and be in all respects a truly All-American Girl."

At one point, Bonnie Baker got a chance to thank Philip Wrigley in person. In the midst of 1943 spring training, after an early-morning Charm School session and a couple of hours at the hairdresser ("They dolled me up and I had a sort of upsweep"), Baker went to the ballpark and reported to Ken Sells, the League president, who led her to Wrigley's box seats. "The closest I had ever got was chewing his gum," says Baker, "so I was quite excited. But when I took my mask off, my hair was hanging down. It was one of the most embarrassing moments of my life." Sells assured her that it didn't matter, and introduced her to Wrigley and his wife: "And they were very nice, very ordinary kind of people. I thanked him kindly for starting the League because it had been one of my dreams to play professional ball." This was the only time that Baker and Wrigley met—and one of the very few times he saw a player in the flesh. Years later, he confessed to a reporter that he never saw an All-American team in action. He knew, he said, that he'd have been disappointed, because he wouldn't have been able to stop comparing the players to men.

And how were things unfolding in the founding cities? Kenosha was pretty representative. The Kenosha *News* was stressing the players' femininity just as much as Wrigley could wish. Just before spring training began, it was running banner headlines such as "Tom-Boy Tactics Out-of-Bounds in All-American Softball League." The story quoted Ken Sells to the effect that "a player is a public entertainer whether in the theater or on the ball diamond and has a definite obligation to the audience to be personally attractive as well as put on a good show." Mme. Rubinstein pops up again: "Women can be athletes, and still be feminine and charming, and therefore a double attraction. Men do not want to come to see women in athletic competition who look like men. A woman who knows how to look, act and walk like a lady is always a Queen whatever her realm."

A couple of weeks later, just before the season opener in June, the *News* was running display ads, complete with a picture of a fielder stretching to catch a line drive, whose copy was indicative of the drums being beaten in every All-American city: "A New Sports Thrill for Kenosha! See America's Greatest Girl Softball Players! Enjoy America's Newest National Sport! It's Carefree, Exciting, Clean Fun! Come out and have the time of your life! Watch these nationally famous girl professionals— the greatest players from the United States and Canada—compete in fast, exciting softball. Watch these girls take their rightful place in the American Sports World, as women are doing in hundreds of other fields. You'll forget your cares— enjoy yourself so completely that you'll go back to work refreshed and cheered. Cheer for Your Own Kenosha Team! Make it a Date and Bring the Family." This stirring copy was provided by the League's head office.

Over the years, almost every national magazine, including *Colliers*, *Life* and *Holiday*, would feature coverage of the All-American's progress. In 1943, however, only one publication marked its launch—complete with minor reservations. *Time* covered the League's opening week of regular-season play in June. It managed to get two out of the four team names wrong (welcoming the "Rockford Teachers" and the "Kenosha Shamrocks"). Otherwise, its copy delivered all that the League could have asked for, saluting Wrigley's attempt to sign up only players of the most sterling character. Women softballers, the author said, had a "hoydenish" reputation and were given to a "special brand of umpire-baiting." It quoted "the dean of girl softball umpires," a man named Harry Wilson, who complained that a catcher had addressed him as follows: "Listen, big boy, if you'd take your lamps off the batter's knees long enough to look around, maybe you'd see more of these pitches coming over as strikes." The League's uniform was heralded as suitably digni-fied, but with an element of the "provocativeness of a Sonja Henie skating skirt." Nonetheless, *Time* felt that these advances might be insufficient, and cited a double-header played between South Bend and Rockford, during which, "despite Helena Rubinstein and Mr. Wrigley, two of the ladies got into a fish-wife argument that nearly ended in a fist fight."

And so the League was formally underway. Its first games were tied to patriotic themes; men and women in uniform were admitted free. Occasionally late-night contests (with an 11 p.m. starting time) were scheduled to suit workers coming off the evening shift. Players began each game by marching into a "V for Victory" formation along the first and third base lines. All across the United States, baseball was firmly linked to war, although major-league owners had considered and rejected the idea of having an army sergeant drill each team before the games got underway, a common practice during World War I. (In Yankee Stadium, the program contained spe-cific Air Raid Regulations. "Mayor LaGuardia has provided a system of safety for patrons attending ball games," it said. "This park is not bombproof but is as safe as elsewhere.")

In July, an all-star game between two All-American teams took place at Wrigley Field in aid of a Red Cross recruiting drive. One squad was composed of players from Racine and Kenosha, the other from Rockford and South Bend. In fact, two games were slated. The first was a lopsided contest, won 16-0 by Peaches/Blue Sox players. This game was notable for several reasons. For one thing, it was the first ever played at Wrigley Field under lights. Few people knew that Wrigley, despite his fear and loathing of night games, had bowed to the inevitable by ordering a set of lights for his Chicago stadium back in 1941. On December 1, they had arrived, and workmen were on the verge of hooking them up when, on December 7, the news came in from Pearl Harbor. On December 8, Wrigley sent his brand new equipment to the government. Now, however, he had relented once again in a good cause, and rigged temporary floodlights atop the grandstands. Dorothy Hunter remembers that the effect left much to be desired. "You were lucky if you could see who was sitting next to you," she says. "The outfielders were dead ducks; the ball went up in the air and they didn't know where it was." Due to a lengthy between-games program starring Victor Mature, the latest Hollywood sensation, the second contest was called after three innings, everybody went home, and Wrigley Field returned to the dark ages.

How were the players received in their team cities? The local sports fraternities were instant converts—if only because they had a good thing going. The League ensured positive coverage by hiring newspapermen as scorekeepers and announcers. What seems to us an obvious conflict of interest today was then standard practice, even in the major leagues. Many a sportswriter confessed that his initial doubts vanished when confronted by the quality of play. But this did not guarantee local enthusiasm, and a couple of teams had difficulty getting off the ground. The Kenosha Comets were a case in point. Placed in the League's smallest city (its population was less than 50,000), they suffered through a "slow, coaxing start." One fan complained in a letter to the editor of the local paper that "the girls are playing their hearts out for a town that simply will not back them, except when people can get free tickets. Then the stadium is jammed beyond capacity." Kenosha, he concluded, was rife with "pikers."

But the city rallied, launching a major campaign in which businesses sponsored individual games, offering war bonds as prizes. One night, 200 firms put up $1,000 in awards, drawing a crowd of 1,800 people. The next night, that number was bettered in response to another promotion mounted by the Chamber of Commerce. Then the Veterans of Foreign Wars sponsored a game that saw the Comets host the Rockford Peaches. The VFW's drum and bugle corps played martial tunes while a special train unloaded 100 employees from Milwaukee's Chain Belt Company, where Eileen Burmeister, a Rockford player, used to work. Slowly, these and other innovative promotions took hold, and the League's morale-boosting mandate was fulfilled. Kenosha's attendance surged. By season's end, the Comets had attracted 60,000 people to their home games—drawing fans not only from their own town but also from nearby Racine.

The 1943 season ended with Racine atop the standings, thanks in part to Johnny Gottselig's managerial expertise. The Belles went on to win the championship, beating Kenosha in three straight games. The players went back to their homes, families and regular jobs. And Wrigley, on balance well pleased with the initial success of his enterprise—176,000 fans for 108 games—sat down to make plans for its immediate future, plans that would threaten to finish the All-American before it had really begun, and which would contribute to his withdrawal by the time the 1944 season was out.

1944

✕

CALIFORNIA GIRLS AND "THE SILVER EAGLE"

Pepper Paire was nine years old when she first began to play organized softball in Depression-era Los Angeles. It was 1933, when unemployment and poverty were at their peak. Pepper's first neighborhood team was sponsored by Sattinger's Grocery Store. "If we won, I got to go to the grocery store, get a brown bag and put as much as I could into it. So I learned real early that it was valuable to win."

Paire was one of the Californians who descended on the League in 1944. They were brasher and cockier and more sure of their abilities than most of the other players. They seemed as different from the other Americans as the quieter, meeker Canadians did. Illinois must have come as a rude surprise. In California, practices were held on the beach at Malibu—a far cry from the city parks of the midwest. But California, despite its sophistication, was just as softball-mad as anyplace else. Major studios such as Paramount and Columbia sponsored teams. Stars like George Raft (who specialized in gangster roles, and kept refusing the parts that made Humphrey Bogart a star) and Burgess Meredith hung around having their pictures taken with the players. In fact, Wrigley had seriously considered transporting the League's teams to L.A. for a season of winter ball in 1943. But for various reasons—among them, residency problems for the Canadian players, who would have had difficulty obtaining year-round work permits—it didn't pan out.

By early 1944, Wrigley had settled on the League's next two new centers of operation—Milwaukee, Wisconsin, and Minneapolis, Minnesota, where local backers signed up to support, respectively, the Chicks and the Millerettes. These schemes—in which Wrigley took a personal hand—would very shortly prove disastrous.

Just prior to spring training, 1944, however, the League's future looked bright, despite one or two problems with player allocation. Wrigley's original notion—to return everyone to a central pool and distribute them afresh each year—had already fallen by the wayside. The 1943 season had shown that local fans quickly became attached to favorite players, either because of their winning personalities or specific skills. If a team lost a popular player, it lost a guaranteed ticket-seller. The League therefore decided on a compromise. Each team could keep a core of players from the previous year but would throw the rest of its roster back into the pool. That would still leave plenty of room for trading. But that wasn't the end of it. Mid-season injuries took their toll. If a top-ranked player was benched, her team would expect the League to supply it with someone of equal skill. There weren't any farm teams, so replacements had to come either from spring training rejects or (under protest) from another club. Most organizations wound up feeling hard done by, sometimes with strong justification.

Meanwhile, some of the Chicago teams that Wrigley had raided were setting themselves up as the National Girls Baseball League, which was neither national nor baseball; it was the same old grab-bag of teams, who continued to play softball.

They were, however, prepared to give Wrigley a taste of his own medicine by trying to raid his players. This development consolidated a pattern of mutual raiding that would last for years, and give the All-American's top-ranked players a threat to use when negotiating their contracts. If the All-American wouldn't meet their price, they had an alternative employer for their skills.

Having skimmed all the players he wanted from Chicago, Wrigley now needed thirty new faces for the two expansion teams. His scouts had been beating the bushes all winter long. One of their most promising acquisitions was Connie Wisniewski, a blonde, Polish beanpole from Detroit, who had perfected a dramatic "windmill" pitching style (full-arm rotation, like a ferris wheel) by throwing balls through a tire suspended from a tree. She was living with a mother who was 100 percent against her going anywhere: "She was from Poland, very old-fashioned," says Wisniewski. "She said only bad girls left home. There was no way she was going to let me go. I told her that if I didn't go with her blessing, I'd go without, and join the army for three years. She asked me how long these ball games were going to take, and I said they'd take three months." Wisniewski was back five months later, and played ball every summer for ten years thereafter.

After the first season, Wrigley's scouts branched out as publicity of a successful summer spread. The Californians were brought in en masse by Bill Allington, who had managed women's softball teams in L.A. and would later in the season begin a long League career as manager. The first six players he brought from California were Alma "Gabby" Ziegler, Faye Dancer, Pepper Paire, Dorothy "Dottie" Wiltse, Annabelle Lee and Thelma "Tiby" Eisen. Allington preceded them, and was waiting at Chicago's Union Station. "Gosh," he said, "you gals have an awful lot of luggage here for two weeks." Allington knew full well that all of them would make the League. But

Ziegler, a wiry little second baseman who became the spark-plug of the Milwaukee Chicks, remembers that they worked themselves hard: "We wanted to make an impression. I got a terrible blister on my foot, and Faye Dancer wanted to cut it off. To show you how dumb I was, I let her. She used a pair of scissors. Everybody thought I was crazy, and it didn't help much. But I made the team." In fact, all of them proved to be first-rate ball players, boosting Allington's reputation as a man who knew baseball talent.

As for Pepper Paire, she found the prospect of playing ball all summer long—and getting paid in cash, not groceries—appealing. "We thought we'd died and gone to heaven," she says. Paire was undaunted by the midwest's less than temperate conditions. The stocky redhead, who became one of the League's most reliable catchers, was also its balladeer. It was she who wrote the All-American's hummable "Victory Song," which players sing today at their reunions.

Paire's first season was fraught with peril. She was assigned to the Minneapolis Millerettes, in whose service she collided with a Racine Belles player, thus fracturing her collarbone. Racine was much criticized for this, because the Belle was attempting to score an unimportant run, late in a game that Minneapolis had plainly lost. The injury forced Paire to spend most of the season recuperating, along with Faye Dancer, who had cracked a vertebra by running full-tilt into one of her fellow Minneapolis outfielders in pursuit of a fly ball. The invalids spent most of the schedule in Kenosha, appearing often in the stands with players from the Comets, another team riddled with injuries. If you were out of action, the League's rule against fraternizing with opposing players was temporarily waived.

When firing on all cylinders, however, Paire maintained an active social life. "I had a boyfriend in every port," she once recounted. "Only one time did I ever get caught. This was in the days of gas rationing, so you didn't expect to see someone you knew in one town show up in another. But in this game in Grand Rapids, one of my teammates and I looked up, and there sat four guys we knew from elsewhere. Well, that type of thing wasn't done in our day, but we handled it like big-lea-guers. We hid under the grandstand."

And what of Dancer, who'd performed emergency surgery on the luckless Gabby Ziegler? Her exploits were many and varied. Dancer was a talented outfielder whose pranks on and off the field threatened to overshadow her baseball career. She talks like a wound-up toy. "My brother says I always sound like I've been vaccinated with a phonograph needle," she jokes. This very brother was fighting in the South Pacific when Dancer entered the League, but she figures that their mother "got more grey hairs over what I did."

Dancer was a pretty, freckle-faced blonde gypsy, moving from Minneapolis to subsequent expansion clubs, first Fort Wayne and later Peoria. One of her most notable eccentricities was her collection of glass eyes, which she liberated from blameless taxidermy in bars while her accomplices created a diversion. She turned cartwheels in the outfield, performed swan dives into mud puddles just because she felt like it, and once called time, either because she wanted a drink of water, or had swallowed a lightning bug, or possibly both. Most people were at a loss to describe her and settled for "colorful." Not surprisingly, spectators loved her. Dancer's theory was that "the fans paid my way. So I always tried to involve myself with them, in every town we went to. I wanted to have fun, and I wanted people to feel like they were getting their money's worth." And so they were—especially since Dancer's eccentrici-ties were founded on real talent. She won the nickname "Dan-gerous Dancer" when she helped skunk the Chicks by blasting two home runs into their left-field bleachers, a feat no other player in the League had managed.

Dancer also consorted with doubtful characters. In Fort Wayne, she befriended a midget, whose lot in life was to bring the players beer. In Peoria, a "gentleman of no fixed income"— a gangster—took a shine to her: "He and his friends had seats right above the dugout. He drove a blue bulletproof Packard to all our road games." The suitor attempted to persuade Dancer to stay in Peoria year-round by promising to establish her in business and buy her a palomino horse, but she refused. California beckoned. This didn't deter her admirer. He threw parties for her at his home, which was guarded by armed henchmen. When her parents arrived from California to see her play, the hoodlum obligingly laid on a series of entertainments, both at his house and at a local night club.

Dancer was also known to play the field. Another swain, who acted as the team's groundskeeper, presented her with a diamond ring, but she had the stone removed and mounted in a nicer band. Neither he nor the mobster got, as it were, to first base. "I wasn't interested in either of them," she says.

To make time for these activities, Dancer kept late hours. One night, after a particularly intensive celebration, she returned to her hotel well past curfew and spotted Ken Sells sitting in the lobby with a posse of chaperons. Dancer's solution was to stack several beer barrels on top of a coal pile, which enabled her to reach the fire escape. She then managed to slice her way in through a screen with a nail file and get cleaned up before anyone could accuse her of the prank.

One of Dancer's main concerns was the All-American's uniform. Californians had always played in shorts, "and we kind of resented these dresses. But after half a season, I enjoyed them. I took tucks in the skirt, rolled the socks down and played with the bill of my cap up," (thus anticipating the Minnesota Twins, who brightened the 1991 World Series by twisting their hats into shark fins!) Plainly, Dancer—along with other recruits such as Merle "Pat" Keagle, who was known as "The Blonde

Bombshell" and "The People's Choice"—would bring sparkle to the All-American's crucial second year of operation.

Wrigley's high hopes for his new teams, the Minneapolis Millerettes and Milwaukee Chicks, were almost immediately derailed, for several reasons. A glance at the map reveals one problem facing the Minneapolis team: it was 400 miles from Rockford, Illinois, the nearest League town. Minneapolis represented a nightmare for League schedulers and opposition teams, who arrived surly and exhausted after a marathon journey.

The League realized their folly within weeks and folded the franchise. Rather than disband the team, however, Wrigley kept it going throughout 1944. Its members became known informally though accurately as "the Orphans." They lived in hotels and played nothing but on-the-road games, wandering the countryside with their manager, Claude "Bubber" Jonnard. Dancer and Jonnard did not see eye to eye. She remembers she "hated him with a passion" because of his play-it-safe style. He didn't gamble for extra-base hits. His runners were instructed just to get on board; the next batter could bunt her along. Dancer's technique was at odds with Jonnard's conservative approach: "I liked to play wide-open, hard-sliding but clean. So I ignored him. I just ran on my own, and if I knew an outfielder didn't have a good arm, I wouldn't even slow down, I'd just keep going."

In 1945, the Minneapolis Millerettes were adopted by Fort Wayne, Indiana. Renamed the Daisies, they lasted in one form or another till the very end of the League.

Milwaukee, the other new franchise in 1944, also had problems. It was accessible enough—a short drive beyond Racine and Kenosha. The city also supported the Milwaukee Brewers, then a Double A team, providing exactly the situation that Wrigley had originally envisioned—the League's first chance to place a team in a large city to play in a regular baseball stadium.

But Milwaukee did not embrace girls' baseball. Local sportswriters adopted a "show me" attitude, and fans weren't encouraged to come out and watch. The Chicks were forced to play mostly daytime games, because the Brewers moved in at night, effectively limiting the number of potential spectators.

The ticket price for All-American games—a dollar, the same as for the Brewers—was regarded as too high, but Wrigley refused to cut the price. He felt that a reduction would admit defeat and reinforce the idea that girls' baseball was second-class. Instead, in a bizarre decision, he chose to boost attendance by hiring the Milwaukee Symphony to play a program of classical music prior to the Chicks' home games. In a memo, he urged the team's backers to mount "a complete show, a woman's show. If people feel our price is too high, we can say fifty cents is for the show and fifty cents is for the game."

The symphony orchestra failed to draw the crowds. The Milwaukee *Journal*'s sports editor summed up general reaction to the program thus: "Mr. Wrigley's minions hope that the music lovers who attend the concerts will not get up and walk out when the girl ballplayers take the field. Mr. Wrigley's minions, confidentially, think he is nuts, but they would not be quoted for anything—not because P.K. would fire them (he is not that way at all), but because they have thought before that some of the millionaire gum man's ideas were screwy and have seen those nutty ideas pay off."

Wrigley finally realized that he was fighting a losing battle in Milwaukee; he had just been handed proof positive that his original concept wouldn't wash. The real problem was that the All-American game, played on a smaller diamond, got lost in the cavernous environment of a big-league park. League President Ken Sells watched the Chicks play, and confessed that "it was a flop. It was awful. We could tell in just a few weeks that it wasn't working. We would go out to the ballpark ourselves and we felt that we were too far away from the ball players." The symphony soon abandoned heavy-duty classics and chugged its way through such accessible melodies as "Tales From the Vienna Woods" and excerpts from *Lohengrin* and *Carmen*. But faced with this cultural hybrid, and the sensation that they were looking at the field through the wrong end of a telescope, fans went elsewhere.

Amazingly, given these conditions, Milwaukee's manager, Max Carey, had succeeded in molding his Chicks—a name inspired by a popular book of the day, *Mother Carey's Chickens*—into a first-class team. But 1944 would be Milwaukee's only year. The Chicks moved in 1945 to Grand Rapids, Michigan, where they would remain until the League's demise.

This failed attempt at expansion was alarming to League officials, who wanted to make sure fans were getting their money's worth one way or the other. Several changes were put into effect in order to dynamize the game. Scorers were instructed to lower the number of recorded errors when high figures threatened to make the players sound fumble-fingered. In mid-season, a hastily convened gathering of League managers stepped up to the plate themselves in order to figure out why there was such a scarcity of .300 hitters. The Rockford *Register-Republic* reported their consensus that "the dead ball was the problem." The ball size was promptly dropped to eleven and a half inches and the basepath was lengthened, to slow down base-stealing.

This was the first of many tinkerings that would continue unabated until the League disbanded. Their effect was to make the game more like baseball, less like softball. In fact, the League now decided that it could legitimately change its name. In 1944, it became the All-American Girls Ball League. In 1945, it was finally changed to "Baseball."

Pat Keagle's first assignment in the All-American landed her with the ill-fated Milwaukee Chicks, as part of the League's player allocation scheme. When she reported to Max Carey at

Milwaukee's Borchert Field, the team was riddled with injuries. Their left-fielder had sprained an ankle; their sparkplug second baseman had a twisted leg; the third baseman had a sprained finger. The club's performance showed it. The night that Keagle arrived, Milwaukee had lost the first game of a double-header against the Blue Sox, and was lagging woefully in the standings.

Connie Wisniewski was the starting pitcher for the second game. She saw Keagle coming and decided that the stylish blonde was not the answer to Carey's prayers. Keagle was of barely average height. Although sturdily built, she seemed unathletic, perhaps because she'd shown up in best Charm School ensemble. "She had on real spike heels and her hair was in an updo and she had on a fancy silk dress," says Wisniewski. "I thought, 'Oh, my goodness, we're going to lose 20-0 with her in the outfield.'" What Carey thought is not a matter of record, but he got Keagle suited up and ready to go. Far from standing helplessly by, Keagle took immediate control of the game, smacking two singles, a double and a home run. "She was a team all by herself," says Wisniewski. "We started jumping around and hugging her. She knocked in all the runs."

Nor was Keagle quite so unassuming as she appeared. She liked the limelight, and played well to it. On another occasion, when Wisniewski was coaching first base (common practice for a pitcher if her side was up), Keagle was called out at first by the umpire. "She'd been out by about two steps," says Wisniewski, "but she was right in there yelling at him, gesturing with her hands, like she's saying, 'I was safe by this much.' I tried to stop her, because I didn't want her thrown out of the game. But when I got close enough to hear, she wasn't even arguing the play. The crowd was booing the umpire, but she was telling him how big the fish was she caught last week. She was a real crowd-pleaser."

Shored up by Keagle's timely arrival, Milwaukee soon improved its showing to such an extent that the League launched a flurry of baffling player reallocations. The Milwaukee team had captured third place only after asking for and getting better players. Now they looked capable of going much higher in the standings, and so the Kenosha Comets declared themselves in need of immediate help; pitching ace Helen Nicol was out with a bad arm. Rockford's *Register-Republic* riled fans by reminding them that, in response to Kenosha's request, "the League lifted southpaw Mary Pratt from Rockford. So what happened next? Nicol got her pitching arm back in shape, and she and Pratt combined forces last night to sweep a double-header with South Bend and put Kenosha in a tie for first." The League received no thanks from the Comets, who a week later sent a delegation direct to Wrigley to find out why they didn't have an even better pitching rotation.

The upshot was that Milwaukee and Kenosha were the two top clubs of 1944, and played each other for the championship. Milwaukee, which had little local support from fans, won. The problem of an abstract concept (balancing out the teams all season long by means of piecemeal forced marches) at odds with sporting reality (building morale by keeping a team together) continued to plague the All-American at every turn.

For many of the girls of the All-American, the chance to get away from home and seek new experiences was introducing them to worlds they'd never imagined. In spite of the homogeneous image put forward in the All-American's press packages, players came in all shapes and sizes, and some with different sexual preferences. When the twenty-seven-year-old Dorothy Hunter arrived in the League in 1943, she'd "never heard of lesbianism," so her more sophisticated teammates decided to give her the low-down, bustled her into a corner, and spun her suitably lurid tales of the lesbian lifestyle: "They told me they had wedding ceremonies. Well, I just thought they were giving me the gears because I was a green Canadian." At season's end, older and considerably wiser, Hunter returned to Winnipeg and confronted her mother. "How come you didn't tell me such things were going on in the world?" she demanded. Mrs. Hunter could only mumble that she thought that Dorothy knew. "Well," said her daughter, with heavy sarcasm, "thanks a lot."

The lesbian lifestyle (or, rather, its alleged outward signs) had long been a bugbear in ball-playing circles. When Connie Wisniewski began to pitch in Detroit in the early 1940s, she was told she'd be kicked off the team if she chose to get a close-trimmed haircut. More than one All-American recruit who showed up at spring training with a boyish bob was handed her return ticket before she'd had the chance to take the field. Dottie Ferguson was warned by her chaperon against wearing girl's Oxford shoes, because they were excessively masculine-looking. Pepper Paire endured a "lot of guff" in high school because she played ball. Her well-publicized success, and the publicity that surrounded her taking part in a tour to Mexico City, only made things worse. Even her teachers thought "it wasn't the thing for a young lady to do."

The All-American had lesbianism on its mind, but they didn't choose to meet the issue head-on with plain speaking. By comparison, the rougher-hewn Chicago League, which didn't believe in chaperons, Charm School or double-talk, warned its members explicitly against pairing off. The fear of lesbianism prompted one All-American manager to release two players because he was certain they were lesbians and thought they might "contaminate" the rest of the team. It explains the All-American's manic, ceaseless insistence on femininity at any cost; it constantly protested too much, raising the specter of same-sex preference even when it wasn't there. But homosexuality was as much a part of the 1940s as the 1990s. There were some lesbian players, and, chances are, chaperons. The fact of being lesbian was probably an added inducement to flee the stultifying atmosphere of their home towns and go on the ball-playing circuit.

Many of the stories of lesbianism fail to ring true, but others are attested to by independent sources. Fred Leo, who became the League's publicity director and later assumed its presidency, says that he once discovered that an attractive young recruit was living with a man in a hotel. Confronted, the pair revealed that they were married but had decided to keep the fact a secret. Leo insisted that they announce the marriage, which they did. And that, he thought, was that. Two weeks later, however, he ran into the downcast bridegroom.

"What am I to do, Mr. Leo?" he said.

"What do you mean?" said Leo. "What's the problem now?"

"She won't have anything to do with me," replied the husband. His wife, he said, had tired of conventional wedlock and left him to carry on a torrid affair with one of her female teammates.

"That player converted this young married woman in just two weeks," says a wondering Leo.

Told by Leo about the miraculous conversion, Manager Johnny Göttselig decided he needed proof. He took over room allotments the next time the team was on the road and refused to let the two players room together. They were angry, and complained so vehemently that Gottselig considered it proof they were having an affair. Leo confesses to having forgotten the married player's fate, but remembers that her teammate remained in the League for a couple of seasons.

In yet another instance, a married player was found to be frolicking with a woman unconnected with the team. Challenged by the chaperon, she was not contrite. In fact, she expressed her intention of continuing the relationship. This time, Leo summoned the husband, who came and took her home.

Given these experiences, the best plan was blanket denial. In 1945, Dottie Hunter, by then in Grand Rapids with the relocated Chicks, was approached by Bill Priaulx, the team's business manager, who had become concerned by rumors of too-close friendships. "Not on this team, Bill," Hunter replied, thus easing his mind. Hunter wisely continued to turn a blind eye unless the violations were flagrant. She did, however, take pains when making room arrangements. "I tried to keep the newer girls together," she says, "because I thought the slower they learned about what was going on, the better."

Naturally, the players got matters sorted out among themselves. As Hunter learned during her first season, lesbianism was a perennial topic for speculation on the grapevine. When it came down to cases, older, more mature heterosexual players, even if they were baffled or initially dismayed, accepted lesbian women they liked and respected. Younger, more sheltered recruits had no idea how to handle their new-found knowledge. They feared being approached. Their solution was to make friends with players they knew or felt were "safe," and keep their distance from those whose motives they weren't sure of.

Rumors were fed by the hothouse atmosphere that existed during the regular season. Not only were the players under steady scrutiny by managers and chaperons, they had to contend with host families and landladies, club officials and their curious wives. Privacy was almost nonexistent. Chaperons could give the green light to dates with male admirers, but the theory was that a player's safety lay in numbers. An admirer might find himself squiring not only the object of his affection, but half a dozen of her teammates—an ad hoc watch committee. Few of the All-Americans had steady boyfriends. Six out of seven days were spent in a blur of practices, hard-fought evening games and weekend double-headers. After you won or lost, you usually celebrated or commiserated with your teammates, if you didn't climb aboard an overnight bus. Even if you stayed put, it was curfew before you turned around. There wasn't time to get to know a new face.

Some players were married, with husbands in the service or down on the farm. Several had children. Dottie Collins pitched until she was five months pregnant. When Olive Bend Little gave birth to her first child, Roberta, in 1944, Ken Sells announced that the League had sent "Bobbie" a contract for the 1960 season. Motherhood was fine, a plus when it came to the publicity mill. But husbands seem to have been most appreciated in the abstract, valuable as long as they kept their distance. Roberta Little's father was safe at home, in Poplar Point, Manitoba. Bonnie Baker's married state contributed to her positive image but Maury was far away overseas. She got at least one letter from a fan (also in the service) who'd learned of her exploits in *Life* magazine: "He told me he had two daughters, and hoped they'd grow up to be just like me. That type of thing meant a lot." Pat Keagle's husband was in the service as well, and appeared only when he was on leave, accompanied usually by their toddler son. This made for a charming photo opportunity, after which father and son retired westward.

Other husbands remember feeling almost unwelcome. Don Key (who married Dorothy Ferguson) and Dave Junor (who wed Daisy Knezovich) would come to visit from time to time and tried to make themselves useful. They would act as chauffeurs, or swat balls during fielding practice. These gestures were not appreciated. When Ferguson was mired in a hitting slump, she received an anonymous letter suggesting that she would be better off single, and thus able to keep her mind on the ball. Even when she and Don Key were married, they had to keep the chaperon informed when they went for a postgame dinner with fans.

The Kenosha Comets' Christine Jewett, single and unattached, remembers that "you were discouraged from getting friendly with any of the fellows in any of the towns, even the towns you played in. They didn't want you involved in other things. They wanted your whole attention on baseball." Daisy Junor found this unnatural and stifling. She liked the home in which she stayed because there were men in the family. She would often go dancing with a young male relative who lived next door. These excursions set tongues wagging, although they were strictly platonic. The reason why Junor enjoyed them, she says, is that "I was starved for the sound of a man's voice." It was, after all, 1944, and men were in short supply. Many of the players had fathers, brothers and husbands overseas. Just before a game against the Comets, Dorothy Maguire, a catcher with the Milwaukee Chicks, learned that her husband had been killed in action. A public announcement was delayed, and she insisted on playing, standing in the "V for Victory" formation on a warm June night, knowing that her husband's voice was stilled forever.

When there was bad news to pass on, it was usually the chaperon who did the dirty work. A chaperon did everything that needed to be done, and Milwaukee's Dorothy Hunter was one of the best. She had been a valuable player with the Racine Belles in 1943. Asked to return in 1944, she declined, having decided that twenty-eight was too old to risk life and limb on the basepaths. The League counter-offered with a chaperon's position. Hunter thought about it. She remembered that Racine's chaperon, Marie "Teddie" Anderson, had suffered much: "She was a sweet woman, but the girls could be hard on her." Well, it would be a challenge, and if she didn't like or couldn't take it she could always quit. So Hunter accepted. She joined the Milwaukee Chicks, moved with them to Grand Rapids and stood by her post until the League folded in 1954.

Hunter's no-nonsense manner did not detract from her popularity. If players were too boisterous in the shower room, she would stand at the door and swat them with a metal coat hanger as they came out. On the bench, when the team faltered, she would offer sound advice: "If you put your bats where your mouths are, you'd be good hitters." Hunter was well-liked by everyone—one of the few chaperons who earned the players' sometimes grudging respect by means of a delicate balancing act. "You had to be a certain type of person," she says. "You had to get mad at the right time and laugh at the right time, too. I know why they pulled all those tricks. It kept their spirits up and kept that winning attitude going. I didn't want to squash them too much, because it went along with baseball."

The chaperons tend to get lost in the shuffle of All-American history—the unsung heroines who gave the League its stamp of respectability, a sort of Good Housekeeping Seal of Approval. Underpaid and overburdened, they changed places almost as frequently as managers, which is saying something. Like the players, they too had to contend with peculiar restrictions, including a dress code. At first, they wore a sort of modified team uniform, with a longer shirtwaist dress. Later, this evolved to something very like an airline stewardess's outfit. Debate raged over whether or not they had to be fully jacketed on the field. Chaperons tried to imagine having to struggle into their approved wardrobe before administering emergency first aid to a player laying with a twisted ankle or broken collarbone. The League was nothing if not consistent; it made life hard for everyone.

Given the importance of the chaperon's role, the League was surprisingly perfunctory about recruiting them. The announcement of a chaperon's appointment tended to come out of the blue; the All-American rarely made much of her arrival. In some cases, this is because she simply stayed where she'd been. The chaperon's post frequently went to retiring players, including (besides Hunter) Marge Stefani, Shirley Stovroff, Dorothy Green, Josephine Hagemann and Doris Tetzlaff.

Green, Hagemann and Tetzlaff each spent four seasons on the job, but the others lasted only a year or less. The change from the limelight out on the field to nursemaid in the dugout wasn't one that everybody could make.

Some of those chaperons who were not former players had backgrounds of significant achievement unrelated to baseball. Marie Teichman "Teddy" Anderson, who Hunter remembered from Racine, held world records for the 220-yard dash and the indoor high jump. She'd also tied the records for the 50- and 100-yard dashes, the 60-yard low hurdles and the hop-skip-and-jump. Elizabeth Daily, who went to Peoria, a later expansion city, had served in the Army Nurse Corps, where she was awarded the Bronze Star. The League was not short of grist for the publicity mill, but chose to make little use of it.

And, perhaps, these women were the exceptions. The League very often settled for what it could get, because it wasn't offering all that much. Chaperons received $250 or $300 a month, but this sum was never increased as the years went by. They had no bargaining power; they weren't the stars. Nor could they hope to move from the dugout to a managerial position. Still, life in the All-American was a marked contrast to their only alternative—a high-school gym class in an anonymous town.

Some chaperons were plainly signed up on the strength of their ability to function as feminine role models. South Bend's first chaperon was Rose Virginia Way—a small, birdlike woman with a soft manner and Tennessee accent—who lasted only a year. Other clubs opted for a somewhat sterner image. Marie Timm, who rode herd on the Rockford Peaches for three years, was a former physical education instructor (one of many) who had taught baseball in the school system. Once a club had made its choice—discipline or feminine role model—it continued to hire chaperons of the same stripe. Ms. Way's replacement at South Bend, for example, was Lucille Moore, who lasted four years. She looked like the actress Greer Garson, and would reward the younger players with banana splits if they were particularly successful on the field that day.

In mid-1945, Racine had the good sense to hire Mildred Wilson, from Brooklyn. She had studied physical education at Long Island University and had managed and played catcher for the New York Celtics, a champion softball team. Like Dottie Hunter, her success stemmed from the fact that she'd been there as a ball player. She developed a good rapport with both the team and its manager, Leo Murphy, remaining with the Belles for several years, until she resigned to marry a local doctor.

At first glance, the chaperon's role sounds simple: keep an eye on the players. In reality, it was demanding and stressful. The contract listed twenty-odd separate duties. Most of these dealt with policing the team, but chaperons were also fully responsible for equipment and uniforms. In their home cities, the basic drill included making sure that players attended meetings and Charm School, got on the field for afternoon practice and evening game, and then straggled home by curfew. A certain degree of leeway was acceptable. The theory was that the players would be more or less inhibited in their own backyard, but on the road, the potential for mayhem increased. Chaperons worked almost round the clock, from breakfast wake-up call to late-night bed check (or lonely vigil in the hotel lobby, waiting for stragglers to return).

Road trips were the bane of Millie Lundahl's life. Lundahl was a schoolteacher who signed up to keep the Rockford Peaches under control. Though her father was one of the club's founders, he didn't encourage her to join in, fearing a conflict of interest. He wouldn't go to the board meeting that voted on her hiring. "The night they vote, I'm staying home," he said. When she was hired, he felt that she was starting off with two strikes against her, because the players would assume she was spying for the board. Nonetheless, Lundahl gained the team's trust. "Rockford had the best girls," she says. "They were all very cooperative, they really had baseball at heart."

But Lundahl was in her late thirties, and the hours got her down. "When we were out of town I was rarely free," she says. "It was often two or three o'clock in the morning before I got to bed. After two years, I was exhausted. I'd had no vacation, because the season started before I was out of school. Then, that first year they made the play-offs, school started up in the fall, and I'd have to teach all day and go to the games at night. I was getting too old, as my father said—too old for the swift pitching."

Physical stamina aside, the ideal chaperon was well-groomed, mature and personally charming, with a sense of humor and a knack for coming to terms with fifteen to twenty wildly different players. She was called upon to be tactful or tough as the occasion demanded, and to function as a para-medic when the need arose. Marilyn Jenkins, the Grand Rapids catcher, credits Dorothy Hunter with a host of innovative patch-ups: "She had a heck of a fishing tackle box." She had to know when to waive the rules. Although some chaperons went so far as to call players back to the dugout to apply their lip-stick, Hunter was not among them. She strove to influence the players' off-field behavior and left the rest to luck. "It was hard for them to stay feminine-looking and throw themselves around the field," she says. "But they did it, and they were pretty good. Of course, the minute I was out of sight, they were into their jeans before you could shake a stick. I have a picture of a banquet at the Rowe Hotel in Milwaukee. They threw a big party for us. So I said to the gals, 'Let's look as nice as we possibly can.' Well, very few of them had a pair of heels, and those that did wouldn't wear them. I look at that picture today, and there are half a dozen of them, sitting there in a nice suit with their saddle-shoes and bobby sox."

Some chaperons failed. They were too timid or too rigid, knew nothing about baseball or could not cope with a jungle of cliques and factions. They were supposed to act as confessors and confidantes, to bolster the social skills of shy or awkward players who had difficulty making friends or who needed more than a fast-track Charm School makeover. Others threw up their hands, and decided that, if they couldn't beat the team, they might as well join it. Jo Hagemann, of the Kenosha Comets, could be counted on to see that the back door was left ajar, and accompanied her players to out-of-bounds locales. "We used to sneak off and go to strip clubs," says Christine Jewett. "We just took Jo along." This could have proved expensive. A chaperon was fined along with a player for infringement of the rules. Most of all, in the words of Pepper Paire, "You needed someone who wasn't a fink."

Some chaperons never got past their initiations. These ceremonies fell to such players as Faye Dancer, whose stock techniques included coating the lightbulbs in the chaperon's room with Limburger cheese.

The chaperon's first duty each season was to get the players lodged in suitable accommodation. This meant pre-season visits to prospective homes and boarding houses. Next came the process—fraught with pitfalls—of matching players in their home city and on the road. A fresh-faced seventeen-year-old, away from her parents for the first time, could not be lodged with a hard-drinking, hard-gambling veteran. But birds of a feather bunking together was perilous, too. One year, Hunter had exhausted every conceivable option and was forced to match up as roommates two old hands who liked nothing better than to terrorize the surrounding country-side. This arrangement had hardly been settled when Johnny Rawlings, the team's manager, appeared in a full-blown rage. "What in the hell are you putting those two together for?" he shouted. "Look, Johnny," said Hunter. "Have you got any other ideas? If they're going to kill somebody, let 'em kill each other."

The chaperon had to run interference between players and the manager. The manager, being male, was often ill at ease when it came to intimate details. Once, Hunter had to explain to Rawlings that three of her players had simultaneously started their periods and were indisposed. "What is this," barked Rawlings, "the Red River Valley?" "I was shocked," said Hunter. "I'd never heard that one before."

Hunter—a tall, beautiful brunette of considerable personal charm—was sometimes the focus of flirtatious teasing from admiring managers. She remembers one time when she completely lost her poise. "At spring training, I came out of this building and the men were all sittin' over to one side, while the players were kind of waiting for the bus in the other direction. I saw the managers there so I went the other way and there was a big piece out of the step and I went flyin'. I rolled and I hit the side, and those guys flew down there and tried to pick me up. 'Are you hurt? Are you hurt?' they kept askin'. And I was so mad I said, 'What do you care? It's all your fault.' God, talk about bein' chagrined, I tell you. I was going to be hoity-toity, I'd have nothing to do with them. That sure rained on my parade, so I always remembered that."

The list of chaperon's duties was a long one. Some managers couldn't bear to tell a player she was finished, that she was being traded or released. This fell to the chaperon. Marty McManus, who headed the South Bend Blue Sox, was incapable of wielding the axe, which he thrust instead upon Lucille Moore, who remembers these occasions as the worst part of the job.

As for the managers, their life expectancy in the All-American was short. One writer observed: "The All-American League is the Little Big Horn of the managerial profession." In a sport where the manager was the first to go when his team did poorly, the League earned a reputation for ripping through managers like a buzzsaw—thirty-seven of them in all, not counting the players. "There were a lot of managers we didn't like, and who didn't like us," says Pepper Paire. "For one thing, they were squares. Life goes on and changes, but they didn't."

Mind you, some were pleased to make their escape. The chaperons weren't the only ones to be initiated by the players. Charlie Stis, who spent a very brief spell managing the Racine Belles, lasted just long enough to provide the League with one of its better and oft-told stories. Stis was a mild-mannered man who seemed pretty gullible—tailor-made for a practical joke. The team was on the road and Stis was awaiting the arrival of a couple of new players. Egged on by their teammates, Joanne Winter and Clara Schillace went out of the hotel and returned shortly with two prostitutes, who had agreed to go along with the joke, for a small fee. Clara and Joanne, their teammates nearby but out of sight, knocked at Stis's hotel room door. When Stis answered, Winter spoke up: "Charlie, we've brought you the two new players you've been waiting for." Stis was non-plussed, since the women facing him didn't look at all like All-American players were supposed to. It wasn't until the whole party had gone back downstairs and the manager was about to arrange rooms for his new charges that Winter and Schillace let him in on the joke. After the women left, Stis told his players, "I didn't think they were ball players. They looked like they fell out of a tree."

Wrigley (and Meyerhoff, in later seasons) continued to comb the big leagues for likely managerial talent. Men like Max Carey, Johnny Rawlings and Dave Bancroft brought glamor and the sense of rubbing shoulders with sports immortals when they strode onto the field. Dave Bancroft, who managed League teams in Chicago and Battle Creek, another expansion club, had forty years experience and four World Series appearances as a player with the Philadelphia Phillies and the New York Giants. Josh Billings, who started off with the Kenosha Comets, had spent eleven years with the Cleveland Indians and St. Louis Browns. Leo Murphy's career spanned twenty-five years, many of them with the Pittsburgh Pirates and the Cincinnati Reds. Johnny Rawlings had played with the Reds, the Giants, the Pirates and the Boston Braves. But although some were very good managers, others were not. An illustrious baseball career didn't always guarantee great coaching. Many of them began enthusiastically, but only a few lasted very long or left without a huge sigh of relief on one side or the other.

Sometimes the blame for failure had to rest squarely on the shoulders of the impatient club directors. The men who ran the Kenosha Comets were the worst offenders. They hired a new helmsman every year, except in 1945, when they hired two. By contrast, the Racine Belles, having settled on Leo Murphy that same year, kept him for five seasons; within two, the Belles had won the championship. Johnny Rawlings, at Grand Rapids for five years, tied with Murphy for second place in the longevity stakes. The clear winner was Bill Allington, with eight years in Rockford and two in Fort Wayne, during which time the Peaches topped the standings five times, made the play-off finals eight times and won four championships.

The summer of 1944 was one of the worst seasons for nose-to-nose confrontations involving players, managers, umpires and, occasionally, fans. A few weeks into the schedule, sportswriters began printing a barrage of complaints voiced by unnamed managers about roughhousing players on rival teams. The first serious injury was Pepper Paire's broken collarbone.

Paire was decidedly accident-prone. Worse yet, she wasn't content to pick on players her own size. She chose to tangle with Lou Rymkus, a former professional footballer who'd taken up umpiring for extra money. "He was about six-foot-four," she says, "and he must have weighed 280. I came sliding into second base, and the ball beat me, but I hooked away from the bag. But the second baseman gave me the old phantom tag. She missed me by a foot. Lou was out of position and he called me out. I was lying flat on the ground, and I could see him make the call. I jumped up, but when I landed on my feet he was behind me, still bent over from making the call. I swung around, and my fist hit him square in the chin and knocked him flat. So he's lying there looking up at me, and he says, 'Pepper, I guess you know I gotta throw you out.' And I said, 'Yeah, but dammit, I was safe. She missed me.'"

A short while later, Bert Niehoff, then managing the South Bend Blue Sox, was warned by other managers about the Milwaukee Chicks, whom Max Carey had inspired to heights of aggressiveness. They were trying to make up for a bad first half of the season by pushing for the League pennant in the second half. These warnings were born out almost immediately in the course of a double-header. In the seventh inning of the first game, Gabby Ziegler, the Chicks' captain, was caught between first and second base. Taking a run at second, she flattened lanky Dorothy Schroeder, the Blue Sox shortstop. Schroeder's teammate Lee Surkowski retaliated by flooring Ziegler. Both teams, accompanied by their managers, swarmed from their respective dugouts as umpires struggled to restore order. During the second game, tensions escalated. Two Blue Sox players took turns mowing down the Milwaukee catcher. The first collision knocked her out cold.

The next night, it was Pat Keagle and Bonnie Baker who tangled. Baker had caught a throw from the outfield and tagged Keagle out at the plate before she could retreat to third. "Keagle very plainly gave Baker the elbow after she was called out," a sportswriter reported the next day, "the same elbow first knocking the ball out of Baker's hands and then winding up on Baker's chin." The umpire sided with Baker, but that wasn't good enough. Baker went after Keagle, while Max Carey roared his head off from the sidelines and Niehoff demanded loudly that Keagle be thrown out of the game. Players could always argue that such encounters were accidents. But, as Baker recalls, "You got to know when something was a real mistake."

This incident was Baker's second major brawl inside a month. A few weeks earlier, after Niehoff had been ejected from a game between the Blue Sox and the Kenosha Comets, Baker argued a call with an umpire who threatened to throw her out as well. At the end of the evening, spectators surrounded the umpires as they tried to get off the field, someone threw a punch, and police had to call on the services of a group of navy officers who happened to be attending the game to disperse the crowd and get the officials into their dressing room without serious injury.

Obviously, managers had their crosses to bear—especially those who stayed in touch with their players year-round. Johnny Gottselig spent his winters on hockey skates with the Chicago Blackhawks. The Racine Belles, provided with free tickets, occasionally formed a cheering section. During one closely fought contest, Gottselig eluded the opposition defenseman and set up a clear shot at the net. Just then, the very audible voice of Clara Schillace was heard above the crowd noise, yelling, "Bunt, Johnny, bunt!"

The first example of the League's willingness to blame managers for bad results came about halfway through the 1944 season. The team that started the ball rolling was the Rockford Peaches, who were losing steadily under Jack Kloza. The scene was Rockford's home stadium, in early July. It was Sunday afternoon and time for a double-header. The bleachers were filled with happy families; hot dog vendors plied their greasy wares. The Peaches were playing the Kenosha Comets. If the Comets won both games, they would finish the first half of the season atop the standings. Rockford, on the other hand, would finish fifth in a field of six no matter what the outcome.

One man sat on his own, his elbows on his knees, intent on the scene below. The lone spectator, blue eyes shaded by a Panama hat, was in his early forties, not as old as his white hair might suggest. In profile, his nose was prominent, almost beaky, his face long and tanned.

Down on the field, a thick-set and worried Jack Kloza was acting as third-base coach. He had some of the League's best players under his command, and more than enough experience to run a ball team, but somehow the Peaches hadn't come together. If they had shown sufficient promise and won a reasonable number of games, Kloza would perhaps have been more popular in the clubhouse. As matters stood, his time was running short.

Kloza's problems were compounded by dissension in the ranks. He had hoped to placate the malcontents by allowing the League's head office to assign Gladys "Terrie" Davis, his temperamental center-fielder, to the ailing Milwaukee Chicks. She had not been universally popular, and Kloza saw her departure as a peace offering. That might have worked, but Kloza had then lost Mary Pratt to the Kenosha Comets. Now Pratt was back on the field against her former teammates, as starting pitcher in the second game.

Not that the Peaches, whose roster had been weakened by injuries, had received no help from the League. One of the newer recruits was presently at bat. This was Dorothy "Snooky" Harrell, who had come from Los Angeles. As the man in the stands watched, she stepped into the batter's box, rapped her bat twice on home plate, spat on the handle for luck and then assumed a familiar stance. Harrell had been playing for Rockford for only a week or two, but had already begun to rival the Peaches' leading hitter, Dorothy Kamenshek. None of the

Peaches were at their best today, though. Harrell would come to the plate seven times in the course of two games but fail to get on base.

Late in the evening, the second game wound down and people began to head for the exits. The Comets, who'd won the first game 3-0, were repeating their performance. Both teams would score one more run each, but Kenosha would end up on top. The lone spectator stayed until the last out. He couldn't imagine not seeing a game through to its conclusion. Besides, he wanted to see as much of the Peaches as possible. He was Bill Allington, soon to be christened "The Silver Eagle" by Rockford fans. He had signed a contract to take over management of the Peaches the following week—a development that would not be relayed to Kloza until the following day at a special meeting in Chicago.

When the League issued an announcement of Kloza's "resignation," the public was told that Kloza had "worked himself to a frazzle" and had stepped aside "for the good of all concerned." But too many rumors were in circulation; the clumsy fiction couldn't and didn't last long.

In fact, a story very quickly began to circulate that players from California had engineered Kloza's departure and demanded that Allington replace him. One of the suspects was Snooky Harrell, but she was guiltless. She had been happy to see what she thought was the last of Allington when she left California. His aggressive style struck her as cruel to players and antagonistic to opponents. She believed that his penchant for disparaging remarks had a reverse effect on rival teams: he made a mediocre club mad enough to pull out all the stops and beat you.

In fact, however, there'd almost certainly been a coup of some dimension. At least one player who'd had enough of Kloza's losing ways had held "indignation meetings" in her room to raise support for his ouster. Some players knew (or

thought they knew) that Kloza was doomed a day or two before
he was summoned to Chicago. This gave managers elsewhere
the shivering fits. If players' wishes were taken into considera-
tion by the League, no one was safe. A newspaper reported
that another manager was reportedly "carrying his signed resignation around in his pocket and has been dissuaded from
presenting it to Ken Sells only by the pleas of his club officials."
Whatever the pressure applied to be rid of Kloza, the All-American's managers could not rest easy. The mere fact that they
piloted a losing team was grounds for dismissal.

As for Allington, once he settled into Rockford, Harrell's
reservations seemed unfounded—for a while. "He was really
pretty decent that first year," she says. Rockford's management
certainly thought so. The club made it out of the cellar and
into the first division by the end of Allington's first season.

Allington's virtues and faults sprang from the same
source—he was baseball through and through. He had begun
his career in Kansas and later played professionally with the
Pacific Coast League before he turned to coaching women's
softball. He also worked for the technical department of Twentieth-Century Fox, and would occasionally surface as a bit
player in films, including *It Happens Every Spring*, a baseball picture starring Ray Milland.

Many All-American managers had already settled in the
midwest before they began working for the League, but Allington had family ties in California. He was divorced, but his
teenage daughter lived there with relatives. Nonetheless, the
profile of the League was growing, and Allington was happy to
take on the job of managing the second-division Peaches. It
was the kind of challenge he liked.

Allington was an interesting figure. His strongest endorse-
ments come courtesy of those who never played for him. More
than any other manager, he taught his teams how to play baseball. He insisted on the basics; daily practice was mandatory.

Players were expected to master the hit-and-run, the bunt, the proper fielding techniques, and to do so quickly. On the road, players had a 10 a.m. wake-up call, followed by a team meeting an hour later. The purpose of these meetings was to memorize the contents of the rule book, by means of question-and-answer sessions. After a game was over, aboard the bus heading to the next game, Allington would hold court behind the driver. Every play—winning or losing—would be dissected, every player challenged to justify her performance.

Some managers never discussed a game. Once it was over, it was history. Many players on other teams would have rebelled against such rigors, but Allington took care to select players who wanted to learn, to absorb his expertise. He was an expert talent-spotter. Dorothy Ferguson credits him with exploiting her potential: "I was never a hitter, but I could run and I had a good arm. So he brought those things out in me."

Allington was not liked by everybody all the time. He would stop at nothing to motivate his players; it was his way or the doorway. Dottie Kamenshek says that you learned or cracked under the strain. Players with fragile egos—or rookies, accustomed to small-time success—made painful adjustments, or quit, or asked to be traded. Others, like Kamenshek, weathered the rough patches in return for demonstrable gain. She would stay after practice for additional instruction: "He'd put a handkerchief on the first or third baseline to mark the place he wanted the bunt to stop. And we'd practice for hours to get it there." Kamenshek was left-handed, and Allington taught her to delay assuming her stance until the last possible moment, then drop the bunt towards third and run away from it: "That way, you got two steps toward first before the ball was even on the ground."

But all was not smooth in their relationship. In 1945, Allington cost her the League's batting championship. "I was leading, going into the last two weeks," she says, "and for some reason he came up to me and said, 'So you think you can hit. You haven't learned anything yet.' I suppose he thought it would make me hit better. I think sometimes he thought we'd play better if we were upset. At that point, I wasn't mature enough to take it, and I went right down the tubes." The first year it happened, it crushed her and she slumped dismally. The next year, Kamenshek got mad at him and regained the title.

Snooky Harrell was another player who didn't always see eye to eye with Allington. One day, he loped over to her shortstop position and suggested a way she could avoid making so many errors. Harrell was outraged. "Bill," she said, her voice rising, "I haven't made an error in thirty-five games." It would be longer than that before she stopped stewing over his slight.

Max Carey was another All-American stalwart. After one season as Milwaukee's manager, he became the League's president in 1945. In some ways, it was a shame he left managing. He had been a top-ranked major-leaguer and would later be recognized for his achievements in the Hall of Fame. He was an able manager; the League would find few who could equal his talents.

As president, he would prove an equally able promoter. When things got slow, he could always strong-arm former teammates into seeing a game, producing the requisite I-can't-believe-girls-are-doing-that response. But his grandiose schemes would place him at odds with the club directors. Well-meaning but inexperienced men, they regarded League decisions they disagreed with—and there were many—as personal attacks that threatened their teams and weakened the concept of local autonomy.

Carey was considered one of baseball's immortals, having played seventeen seasons as a center-fielder with the Pittsburgh Pirates. His principal skill had been stealing bases; he led the National League in that department ten times. He was reputed to have perfected the classic lead-off posture—body stooped and hands braced on the knees, ready to break for the next base, or to retreat when the pitcher tried to pick him off. He also set a long-standing record as the only man to reach first base nine times in a single game, a 1922 contest between the Pirates and the New York Giants.

Carey was also a baseball strategist. He knew how to explain his skills to others, how to discipline unruly players. Most of the players regarded him as a father figure. But—unlike Allington—he was not abrasive. Players could include him in practical jokes without fear. Once, Dottie Hunter returned to her hotel room only to find that all her clothes had been replaced with a male wardrobe. "I blew my stack, but there was nobody in sight to direct it to," she says. "So I gathered up all this stuff and went to the elevator steamin'. I go to get in the elevator, and there's Max with all my clothes in his arms. So we mumbled and grumbled and carried on, and you never saw any of the girls again that night. By the next day we'd cooled off and didn't make too much of it, but it never happened again."

Carey had no time for what he perceived as mumbling and grumbling behind his back. He didn't tolerate troublesome players. When Milwaukee was fooling about with the symphony and things looked dark, he rallied the players who'd begun to feel they were second class, that people wouldn't pay full freight to see them, and talked to them in a straightforward manner. "I don't want any dissension on the team," he said. "You have a problem, bring it to me."

Unfortunately, there was another side to Carey's paternalism. Judith Dusanko, a rookie third baseman who'd played on championship teams in the Canadian west, made a strong impression during the 1944 spring training. She was assigned to Milwaukee, but had to ride the bench, because Carey filled the third-base spot with a local player he hoped would draw the fans. Instead of going to him with her dissatisfaction, Dusanko sulked. "Of course, you're pretty dumb at that age, and I didn't go to him—which I should have—and tell him how unhappy I was," she says. "If I had played, and then he'd benched me, it might have been different. But he never even gave me a chance. So this one time in the dugout, I took out my notepaper and stamps and pen and I wrote letters home. Oh, boy. Everything went haywire. He called me right after the game, called me on the carpet in front of everybody, and told me I was off the team. So I went home and cried a lot. I packed my suitcase and I figured I was on my way back to Canada. And I hadn't even had a chance to play."

The next day, Dusanko went to Chicago, to report to League headquarters in the Wrigley Building before heading back home to the Canadian prairies. Here, she was given a reprieve by Ken Sells. "Heck, no," he said. "Who says you're going home? Minneapolis is playing in Rockford tonight and they need a third baseman." Dusanko was driven to the Chicago train station, tossed aboard and arrived in Rockford just in time to get suited up and rush onto the field. But Dusanko's second chance lasted only a single season. When 1945's spring training rolled around, she received a personal letter from Carey, by then the League president, saying there was no room in the League for anyone like her. "It wasn't exactly those words," she says, "but that was the meaning."

An unhappy tale—but most players have pleasanter memories. Tiby Eisen says that Carey handled players well, and was patient even with those recruits who had to learn the basics: "He really made the beginnings of a ball player out of me." He taught Connie Wisniewski to watch opposing pitchers and learn to predict their moves: "He pointed out that they always did a little something just before they threw the ball—a twist of the shoulders, a nod of the head. Maybe it was that their toe turned down. But if you watched for it, you could figure out when they were going to go for home plate, and you could get three or four steps on them."

That was Wisniewski the batter and base-runner speaking. But she was a pitcher, too, and Carey had a lot to teach her in that department. Just before the season opener, he gave the entire pitching staff a lecture on holding the runner. Wisniewski wasn't paying attention. "After a little bit, he said, 'All right, you over there that's talking. You stand up and tell me how to hold them on.'" Wisniewski, a tall and graceful submarine pitcher whose cocky manner masked a painful shyness, decided to fake it. "I'm pitching?" she said. "Well, you tell me how they got on first base with me pitching, and I'll tell you what I'd do about it." This reply appealed to Carey. "He liked that. He said, 'Okay. You're my pitcher tomorrow.'" Wisniewski won that game, but there were one too many stolen bases for her liking, "So I went to him afterwards and asked him to show me how to hold runners." So successful were Carey's seminars that the Milwaukee pitchers managed to put the brakes on even the Racine Belles, who'd stolen twenty-four bases in a single game that year. Unfortunately, when he became president, Carey felt it only fair to attend spring training camp and teach his tricks to all the League's players—which, according to Wisniewski, "took our advantage away."

But this was part of Carey's philosophy. He was a fierce competitor, but he believed in the greater good. He emphasized that baseball was a team sport, although he sometimes failed to follow his own advice. "He used to tell us that we were a team. It was always 'We,' never 'I,'" says Eisen. "But then we'd all go out to dinner and he'd pull out these news clippings of his career and show us what he used to do."

Carey lived in Miami, and he returned there during the winter of 1944, before he assumed the presidency. He held numerous press conferences, stressing his conviction that girls' baseball would continue to thrive when the war ended. Asked if the All-American game was as fast and colorful as men's ball, Carey took the reporter's ears off. It was a matter of scale, he said. The All-Americans ran their seventy-two-foot basepaths as quickly as male big-leaguers covered their ninety feet. As a result, the game looked just as fast, which was the important thing. "Why, my good man, it's four times as fast," he said, "and a helluva lot more colorful. Baseball men themselves—executives, players, old-timers—who have seen it are amazed. Not only at the speed and color of it, but at the skill of these girls. I'm telling you that a lot of them perform as gracefully and with as much talent as good men players."

Later, Carey would tell anyone who'd listen that he was happier in his post as president of the League than at any time during his career, that he actually considered the girls' game "much superior to the game I was mixed up in for twenty-five years as a player and coach." Even allowing for an element of hyperbole in his enthusiasm for the organization he was then heading, it was a strong enough endorsement to be genuine.

And so the season ended. The top two clubs—Milwaukee and Kenosha, kept afloat by their respective allocations—met in the play-offs. Carey's Milwaukee Chicks, who had not one iota of local support, won the championship. Attendance for the year had increased by almost 50 percent, up to 260,000 over an extended 152-game schedule. All well and good—but Wrigley was the man who counted, and Wrigley had changed his mind. By now he was out of pocket by at least $135,000 (the seed money for six franchises). Ken Sells, whose job it was to wind up accounts for him at the end of the 1944 season, says it was closer to $200,000 for the two years.

Wrigley had taken counsel with his sources in the government, and decided that the war—by now sweeping through Europe, with the Pacific theater a mopping-up operation— would end sooner than he'd thought. His fellow Wrigley & Co. board members were noisily split over how the gum business should be run. Some argued that, since the public had accepted cut-rate product during wartime, the company could continue foisting it on people when hostilities ended. This to Wrigley was anathema. He resigned as president of the firm, making public the admission that he was "pretty well worn down physically, with a consequent lack of vigor and enthusiasm," but remained as a director. The All-American had become peripheral in his mind—particularly since, if Milwaukee and Minneapolis were anything to go by, his hopes for establishing the League in major-league centers could not be realized. Besides, the threat to men's baseball was passing, and he could return to propping up the Cubs.

Wrigley sold the All-American League for a token $10,000 to his associate Arthur Meyerhoff's Management Corporation. From now on, the League's responsibilities would remain the same—scouting and recruitment, training, player allocation, a publicity package. But these would be provided on a profit-making basis, while the individual clubs remained non-profit and jointly liable for any overall deficit—an obvious conflict that would plague the All-American for many seasons to come.

1945

HOME BASES AND VICTORY OVERSEAS

The All-American's third summer found Arthur Meyer-hoff holding the purse strings, Max Carey elevated to the president's chair and two new clubs in business—the Fort Wayne Daisies (the orphaned Millerettes resettled) and the Grand Rapids Chicks (the ill-fated Milwaukee franchise, name and all).

Spring training, held in another Chicago ballpark because of Wrigley's departure from the League, was the scene for yet another allocation shuffle. Competition for the good players was fierce among the managers, who "almost came to blows sometimes through wanting some specific player," says Dorothy Hunter. But a really wily manager could use other means to get his way.

Shortstop Dorothy Harrell remembers an instance when Bill Allington relied on his wits to get the player he wanted. Harrell had been approached by the League in 1943, but her employer, the Bank of America, was loath to let her go. The following year she had joined the Peaches, where she and

Enjoy a real sports thrill
Something New Something Different
See ROCKFORD'S Own Team At
HIGH SCHOOL STADIUM
All American Girls Professional Ball League

HOME GAMES SCHEDULE FOR ROCKFORD

Major-league owner P.K. Wrigley promoted girls' baseball as a unique game. Organizers saw themselves as the czars of a new sport that they could franchise around the country.

(Courtesy Dorothy Ferguson Key)

At their first spring training in 1943, players wore their softball uniforms and team jackets from home while manager Bert Niehoff gave them some pointers about the new game they would be playing.

(Courtesy Mary Baker)

Left: Chicagoans Edythe Perlick (left) and Ann Harnett were among the first players recruited to the League in 1943. They helped to make the point that girl baseball players could be as feminine as they were athletic.
(Courtesy Helen Nicol Fox)

Right: Almost all the League games were played at night under artificial lighting that left much of the outfield and all of the spectators in darkness.
(Courtesy Dorothy Ferguson Key)

Left: The Grand Rapids Chicks salute the flag during opening ceremonies. Patriotism played a major role in attracting fans, especially during the war years.
(Courtesy Grand Rapids Public Library–Michigan Room)

Left: The League regularly solicited visits and amazed reaction from baseball legends like Cornelius Magillicuddy (center-left), more widely known as Connie Mack, who visited with the Kenosha Comets when Philip Wrigley was still in charge.
(Courtesy Fred Leo)

Right: The pitching staff of the Grand Rapids Chicks. Connie Wisniewski (center) was one of the great windmill pitchers in the League. Fans loved to come and see her marvelous windup. From left to right, Betty Tucker, Mildred "Mid" Earp, Wisniewski, Alice Haylett, Annabelle "Lefty" Lee.
(Courtesy Betty Tucker)

Left: In the early years, players never wore baseball helmets. Pitchers with speed, but little control, were justly feared by batters.
(Courtesy Grand Rapids Public Library–Michigan Room)

South Bend player
races a throw to first.
Is she safe?
(Courtesy Fred Leo)

In the locker room, after the game and away from the sight of fans and official
the "Charm School girls" of the League could be a little more informal. Fron
row, left to right, Rockford Peaches Lorraine Fischer, Dorothy Ferguson,
Dorothy "Kammie" Kamenshek. Back row, left to right, Mary Pratt, Naomi
"Sally" Meiers, Cartha "Ducky" Doyle. *(Courtesy Dorothy Ferguson Key)*

Right: Alma "Gabby" Ziegler was always a great morale-booster for the Grand Rapids Chicks. She was the Chicks' only captain in the eleven years she played for the team.
(Courtesy Grand Rapids Public Library–Michigan Room)

Left: Some players found the League's dress code too strict to be followed absolutely.
(Courtesy Fred Leo)

Right: Mary Rountree, Peoria Redwings catcher. Rountree was one of a handful of players asked, at various times, to fill in when a team suddenly lost its manager.
(Courtesy Betty Tucker)

Players weren't shy
about challenging an
umpire's call.
Rockford Peaches
Alice Pollitt, Dorothy
"Snooky" Harrell
and Charlene
Barnett argue with
the umpire.
(Courtesy Time-Life)

Havana, 1947. Chaperon Dorothy Hunter (center, wearing sunglasses) and
players listen intently as manager Bill Allington gives some pre-practice
direction while Cuban fans look on.
(Courtesy Grand Rapids Public Library–Michigan Room)

Left: Chaperons had to be able to treat the many injuries the players were prone to, like the one caused by the "beanball" that felled this Muskegon player. *(Courtesy Grand Rapids Public Library–Michigan Room)*

Right: Like all the players, Lavonne "Pepper" Paire, catcher for the Chicks, regularly played with injuries. *(Courtesy Fred Leo)*

w: Opa-Locka, 1948. Every spring train- attracted hordes of still and newsreel otographers who couldn't get enough ictures of the athletic young women. *urtesy Grand Rapids Public Library–Michigan Room)*

Mary "Bonnie" Baker
played for the South
Bend Blue Sox for
eight years before
being moved to the
Kalamazoo Lassies to
fill in for a fired man-
ager. She made it a
winning team and the
club wanted her back
for the following year,
but the League said no
and passed a resolu-
tion against any more
women managers.
(Courtesy Mary Baker)

Clubhouse conditions
varied, but locker
rooms were always
steamy and generally
cramped.
(Courtesy Alice Udall)

teammate Dorothy Kamenshek, the All-American's premiere first baseman, began to forge their fabled double-play collaboration. Harrell recalls the arrival at spring training of Kay Rohrer, a California catcher who immediately became the object of a typical Allington maneuver. "Kay was so knowledgeable and had the greatest throwing arm I think I've ever seen," says Harrell. "She was a great player and Bill knew it—he'd seen her play before. Well, when she was assigned to practice with our team, he didn't play her as a catcher. He put her in the outfield." Harrell is certain that Allington deliberately made sure Rohrer couldn't display her talent. Rohrer came to Rockford, and did much to fulfill Allington's hopes of a better showing.

The customary thirty or forty rookies—touted, as usual, as the best yet—were parceled out, with fingers crossed. Clubs always seemed to be wanting more good players, but the shortage was still not seen as a serious problem. When Carey became president, he swore that he would step up training and recruitment.

The League's publicity apparatus—now controlled totally by the astute Meyerhoff—was working overtime. Pathé and Cinetone News produced lively short features on the All-American's activities, which played in movie theaters nationwide. Coverage continued unabated in the national press. It turned up such prospects as star-struck autograph-seekers and the occasional bedraggled runaway, who got her photo opportunity and was shipped back home to mother.

The trouble was that, even in 1945, the League was becoming hard to break into. As Connie Wisniewski points out, it was almost impossible to become a full-fledged player in two short weeks. Instead, "you rode the bench," she says, "and a lot of these girls that were picked were the best their little cities or towns had to offer. They didn't like that, and I don't blame them. But people weren't going to pay money to see you learning to play baseball. They wanted to see a team that knew how to play." In the early years when the game was still being played on a relatively small diamond, players had a better chance of making it in two weeks. As the game moved closer to baseball, it took softball players longer to adjust.

Carey and Meyerhoff had attempted to alleviate the shortage by various means. They put much thought into the creation of alternate leagues. One, in Canada, would have involved Toronto, Hamilton, London and Brantford. Given the success of the All-American's Canadian players, it seemed like a logical step, but it came to nothing. Carey tried to set up a winter league in Florida, where he had a permanent home. He dispatched Fred Avery, the All-American's general manager, to negotiate with several Florida owners, but Avery pushed too hard and put their backs up. The Florida promoters responded by pulling out of the negotiations, leaving Meyerhoff and Carey to hold wider-ranging (though ultimately fruitless) talks with promoters in New York, Alabama and several Latin American countries. None of these panned out, with the exception of the Latin American contacts, which would eventually result in a quagmire of double-dealing and disorganization.

The League also tried to solve its problems by hiring more scouts. In 1945, it budgeted $7,000 for this purpose. It wasn't sufficient. The so-called scouting network, which never really materialized, dwindled into something called the Commissioner System—a series of one-shot finder's fees payable to anyone who turned up a promising body. That didn't work, either. The best recruiter the League had was the promise of a full-time, fully professional career in "the Glamor Loop," as the League was sometimes called. When the League's reputation began to fade, so did its chances of renewing itself, and it turned inwards, building up new teams while weakening the old.

Life magazine's description of Rockford called it "as nearly typical of the U.S. as any city can be." It lay ninety miles southwest of Chicago—far enough away from the metropolis that it could sustain its own symphony orchestra, a radio station and ten movie houses. Seven trains pulled into the railway station daily. Every Saturday morning, farmers poured in from the surrounding countryside to shop, while their kids roller-skated at a rink across the street from the AFL-CIO office. But on summer evenings, an appreciable number of its 100,000 citizens had only one destination—the ballpark, located on Fifteenth Avenue, and known to one and all as The Peach Orchard.

Fred Leo remembers the first time he saw the Peaches play. It was on the Fourth of July weekend, in 1945. He had been sent (much against his will) by his employer, who owned a radio station in Peoria, which was then debating whether or not to get behind an expansion team. "This infuriated me," says Leo, "because I was against the idea of girls playing anything."

Leo and several potential Peoria backers got the grand tour. Their first stop was the country club, for a game of golf and a meeting with Bill Allington. That was a fairly positive omen; they'd heard all about him. "I thought they were doing a real good sell job on us," says Leo. "But later, when we went for lunch, people were talking about whether this girl's arm was any good, whether that girl was ready to start. I thought to myself, 'They're carrying this thing a little too far.' But as we went to the ballpark that night, there were people waiting at each of the bus stops. And when we got there, the park was overflowing with fans. I saw two fine games, and it really changed my attitude."

The country club set would have given Leo only one impression of what made Rockford tick. A third of the city's inhabitants were of Swedish descent, followed by Germans and Italians. While the privileged gathered at country clubs such as the Maun-Nah-Tee-See or the Forest Hills, small businessmen joined the Chamber of Commerce or fraternal organizations like the Knights of Columbus or the Loyal Order of Moose, and the Italian working man had his St. Mary's Society. Residences of the well-heeled spread along the east side of the Rock River. Heavy industry and humbler homes found room for themselves on the riverbanks to the south. One of the very few places that everyone met on more or less equal terms was in the ballpark—a high school stadium designed for football. The ballpark was on the tonier side of the river, located amid a patchwork of parks the city had cultivated to complement the rolling, wooded landscape.

Rockford's sporting associations were long-standing. In the 1860s, it had been home to the Forest City Nine, an amateur men's baseball team whose roster included A.G. Spalding. (Spalding would become the foremost promoter of his day and build a sporting goods empire by providing balls free of charge to the major leagues in return for having them designated "official" equipment.)

Rockford's support for the Peaches surprised some people. It didn't have a reputation for supporting losing teams, and the Peaches hadn't started to make a good showing until Allington came on the scene; they won their first pennant in 1945. Nevertheless, the people of Rockford were fascinated by the idea of wholesome females playing great baseball, just as Wrigley had hoped they would be. The Peaches—like the Comets, the Blue Sox and the Belles—had sold countless war bonds, enabled factory workers to let off steam and had become a part of the city's social fabric. Local shopkeepers supported the club, rightly sensing an advertising opportunity. Programs and yearbooks sold everything from sewing machines to nights out at the bowling alley. Everybody wanted to get aboard, including people with a couple of rooms to rent. Peaches players were housed, if possible, with families who lived close to the park. They walked to the field, meeting fans who came early to secure a good seat and watch them warm up. At the brick ticket booth sporting the sign "Home of the

Peaches" they separated—fans to stand in line, Peaches to descend to cramped locker rooms beneath the bleachers where the chaperon waited with freshly laundered uniforms.

Each of the All-American's four founding cities had some variant on Rockford's mix of ethnic and social groups united around civic-minded enterprise. Each was large enough to respond to a call for community involvement, yet small enough that community interest could be defined and appealed to. This was the winning formula that Milwaukee and Minneapolis had lacked.

In Grand Rapids, the self-styled "Furniture Capital of the World," things were somewhat more cosmopolitan. Now that Milwaukee and Minneapolis had fallen by the wayside, it was the largest city in the All-American. Its population was 175,000—almost double the size of Rockford. It was wealthier, having been settled by thrifty Dutch settlers whose descendants maintained an allegiance to traditional Christian values. This was made plain to the Chicks when they arrived, fresh from the wicked city. "In Milwaukee, there was a beer garden on every corner," says Connie Wisniewski. "In Grand Rapids, there was a church." Indeed, the Chicks' arrival had been less than auspicious. Their train was met by a local nay-sayer, who informed them that, if they planned to play on Sundays, they needn't bother to unpack their bags. "You'll be gone in a week or two," he predicted.

Fortunately, the Chicks came equipped with Dottie Hunter, who feared neither man nor beast. "If you're our welcoming committee, forget it," she said. "Goodbye. We'll find our own hotel. We'll take care of everything."

Before too long, the doubter was forced to apologize a hundred times over. "The people who didn't want to come on Sunday gave their tickets to somebody else," says Wisniewski. "We really had crowds." A Roman Catholic priest became a fan, and passed the message along to his parishioners. Some of the players began to attend a Methodist church, whose minister had a phone-in radio program and talked about the Chicks at every opportunity. These ecumenical blessings did much to ensure success. "They were all thrilled with us that first year," says Hunter. One day, the owner of the Coca-Cola bottling plant flagged down the team bus in transit and presented the players with cases of his product, unloaded from the trunk of his car.

Others rewarded the All-Americans in more lucrative ways. The Chicks played at South Field, another former high school park. It was rather small, and its right field was drastically foreshortened by the presence of the Dexter Lock Factory. These surroundings made for player-spectator contact. When one of the Chicks hit a home run, she never headed to the dugout after touching home plate. Instead, she cruised the first-baseline stands. "Here were all these guys standing up with their hands out," says Hunter, "and you wanted to shake hands with them, because you never knew what you were going to bring back." Inez Voyce, a left-handed hitter who gloried in the shortened right-field boundary, made a thousand dollars just from handshakes after hitting home runs.

But even those players who didn't receive four-base tips liked South Field. It's still there, untended now and overgrown with weeds, but you can see why it was fun to play in. It's on an appropriate scale; everything seems to fit. People sitting in the back rows must have felt that they could almost reach out and touch the basemen.

Marilyn Jenkins began playing with the Chicks in 1951, but she was only eleven years old when they climbed off the train from Milwaukee. Her father said that he knew she'd want to see them, so she'd better pay her way by going down and getting herself a job: "So I moseyed over and got a job picking stones out of the infield and cleaning underneath the bleachers. The place was kind of run-down at the time. Then this bat girl idea came up, and I was it. I'd come early and shine their shoes, set out the equipment and bring them towels and blankets. I'd take Cokes to the locker rooms." Jenkins' only pay was free admission, but it didn't matter: "To me, it was the greatest honor in the whole city, and it really became part of my life. I was bat girl until I was sixteen. I can remember being there sometimes till late at night and going to school the next morning. My parents didn't mind. They were happy I was into something. Oh, but Dad had come and checked the whole thing out. He talked to Dottie Hunter and the manager, and made sure I wasn't getting into something corrupt and naughty, whatever that might have been back in that time. Then, when I was seventeen, I started playing. It would have been the disappointment of my life had I not become a player."

Meanwhile, the Blue Sox had settled into South Bend, which was dominated by Studebaker, the automobile manufacturer, and by Bendix Aviation Corporation, one of the world's largest manufacturers of airplane parts. Bendix was a city within a city, a forty-five-acre site with paved streets, electric transportation, its own parks system and worker housing built on reclaimed marshland. The Bendix ballpark, however, was too far from the center of town. By 1946, the Blue Sox would move to Playland, a more convenient location that was also used for stock-car races, with the result that a cinder track ran between home plate and the bleachers.

Fort Wayne was a little bigger than South Bend, encircled to the north by a low range of hills, to the south by rich agricultural land. Three rivers converge there, spanned by more than twenty bridges. Fort Wayne is said to have pioneered night ball in 1883, when a game took place, illuminated by the local company that grew up to become General Electric, between a professional team from Quincey, Illinois, and a group of students from the Episcopal college. God was not on the students' side, and the professionals won.

Every All-American city had a unique ballpark. Some had a grandstand; others were simply a diamond enclosed by makeshift bleachers. The only constants were the clouds of pigeons (or gulls, down on the lakeside) and crusty reporters perched in the press box above the grandstand, smoking vile cigars. There was an intimacy to the proceedings, a vulnerability to the elements.

Kenosha's stadium, although it occupied a scenic location on the shores of Lake Michigan, was prone to damp and fog. Lib Mahon, who came from South Carolina, grumbles at her memories of miserable spring weather. "We damn near froze to death," she says. "I remember it snowed once in June, and again in September. We were in the play-offs, and this spritz of snow was coming down." Often, according to Lou Arnold, "You could see your breath out there. Here we were in these short skirts, and the fog would roll in." The fog not only intensified the cold, it enabled the players to pull a disappearing act. Shirley Jameson, the petite center-fielder, was usually the first to vanish in the murk. "All you could see of her," says Dorothy Schroeder, "was from about her ankles on down."

But every park had its drawbacks and charms, its detractors and adherents. Doris Satterfield thought that Grand Rapids' was the best: "We'd take our infield practice, and I'd see somebody in the stands, and they'd wave and say Hi, so I'd go over and talk to them. You got to know each other real well. You couldn't do that with forty and fifty thousand people." Connie Wisniewski agrees: "I loved it. The people were so nice I'm surprised my head didn't get as big as a balloon. They recognized us everyplace; they knew you when you went to mass at church. If you stopped at a restaurant, they made sure you had good seats. No matter what you did, it was, 'Hey, there go the Chicks.' We never got that in Detroit or Milwaukee."

They never got home cooking in Detroit or Milwaukee, either. Every year, the All-Americans settled into their home-city accommodations, vetted by the chaperons. Some were commercial rooming houses, respectable but impersonal. Others belonged to local families, who over the years became almost surrogate parents. In South Bend, the Blue Sox established a second clubhouse at Arnold and Nadine Bauer's.

Arnie Bauer worked at Bendix and was involved with the company's softball teams, along with Ed Deslauriers, who became the Blue Sox business manager. Bendix was to prove a sort of recruiting ground. Another worker, Norris "Gadget" Ward, became the All-American's chief umpire. Ward, at first, would have nothing to do with girls' baseball. The League had taken over the field that the Bendix men's team used, putting Ward in a two-year snit. It was Max Carey who finally convinced him to help umpire one or two League games. And once he saw them play, Ward was hooked.

When the Blue Sox came to town, the Bauers were in their early thirties, with two young children. They started taking in two or three players every season, and Arnie volunteered, first as ticket-taker at the games, then as self-appointed social director: "We'd put on a buffet supper after the Saturday game, for the Sox and the visiting team, if they wanted to come. Most of the time they did. Everyone would sit around on the floor or whatever chairs were available. And, by golly, you never heard such a bunch of magpies. I fixed all the stuff before the game and had it ready for them when they arrived. I started off with potato salad and beans. Of course, this was during rationing, but I managed to get meat, too. I knew the butcher." These impromptu feasts weren't confined to the players. Club officials and the odd fan appeared as well. "And believe it or not," says Arnie, "there'd be policemen come. They'd drop by, have a bite to eat and rehash the game. Then they'd take off in the squad car. We had one on a motorcycle who'd come by pretty near any chance he had."

Dorothy Schroeder didn't room regularly with the Bauers, but she wound up at their place the season she was spiked and

couldn't play. "They took me in and took care of me," she says.
"I wasn't supposed to walk, so Arnie carried me up and down
the steps, all the time I was recuperating." The pretty, pig-tailed
Schroeder brought out people's parental instincts. In Fort
Wayne, where she was later traded, the fans treated her and the
Daisies "just like we were royalty." She remembers two brothers
named Elmer and Arnold Marhenky, who invited the Daisies to
their farm. "They were old bachelors, I suppose in their early
fifties, and they were so generous. They would invite us over for
Sunday dinner, and they were great cooks." And great fans as
well. They kept scrapbooks of the team's achievements. Today,
at her home in Champaigne, Illinois, Schroeder has a table
lamp, handcrafted by the Marhenkys. It features an actual All-
American bat, standing on its tip, with a groove on the base for
a regulation ball.

These and other homes struck reassuringly familiar chords
for the young and homesick. In Kenosha, rookie Christine
Jewett from Saskatchewan would later room with three of her
teammates in one of the neat, ordered neighborhoods not far
from the park. Her house was on the lakefront, and afforded a
view of passing freighters. "The woman's name was Mrs.
McCann," she says. "She'd had teachers staying there for years.
When they left for the summer, we moved in. She was a wonderful old woman, probably about sixty-five or seventy. Every
once in a while, you'd come in and she'd holler at you, and
you'd have to go back into her kitchen. Maybe she'd been
baking something, and she'd make a cup of tea or coffee and
have fancy buns. We'd sit and chat. She was always interested in
us. We could come and go anytime. The front door was never
locked." Jewett was in luck, and managed to keep her homesickness at bay. Except for the passing freighters, Mrs.
McCann's was a good deal like small-town Saskatchewan.

But not every player needed or wanted surrogate parents
baking them fancy buns. Older or married All-Americans

tended to set up houskeeping among themselves. Bonnie
Baker shared an apartment above a Rockford doctor's office
with several of her teammates. Some players wanted merely to
be left alone—impossible, when prowling chaperons were on
the watch. Snooky Harrell, who had managed to secure a car of
her own, remembers that Dottie Green summoned her to the
club office one morning to inquire where she'd been at 12:30
the previous night. Harrell replied that she'd been home, and
wondered why Green thought otherwise. "Well," said Green,
"your car wasn't in front of the house." Harrell, who had found
a garage down the street in which to park her car, was not
amused at the prospect of being monitored in the small hours.

When Pepper Paire heard the story, she could only be
thankful that the assiduous Green was not responsible for
checking up on her. Pepper lived near a cemetery, where she
hosted late-night get-togethers amid the tombstones. She
would provide a six-pack of beer and roam the grounds
("being very careful not to step on the graves") debating issues
of the moment with visiting players and talking to the
departed. Paire's favorite conversation piece was a memorial to
Mrs. Murphy, whose spirit became the recipient of her inner-
most confidences.

Exchanges between team members and their benefactors
could sometimes be a bit labored. Arleene Johnson remembers
that being a Canadian proved useful when conversation
lagged: "This seemed to be something they were interested in.
We'd talk about the weather, the snow. They thought I was
living with the Eskimos. They wanted to know what I did in the
off-season. I curled, but it was hard to explain what that was
unless you could demonstrate. It wasn't enough to say you
threw a rock."

The League played up the stereotypes if it got them publicity. One year, they issued a news release about a Canadian
player mushing by dogsled from her north Saskatchewan home

to the railhead in Saskatoon to catch the train south. Newspapers ran it without a hint of tongue-in-cheek.

Boosting the clubs had become a fashionable exercise for the civic-minded. The local elite helped raise money and bought the more expensive box seats for the season. It was considered chic to dine at the country club, then stroll on down to the park. Once, during a period of high unemployment and lower than usual attendance, Dottie Ferguson's husband suggested that the ticket price be reduced to draw more crowds. The assembled worthies looked at him askance. Such a course, they said, might attract "the wrong sort of people."

The right sort of people stretched the players' social skills with a non-stop round of lunches, picnics and barbecues. This is where Charm School lessons came in handy. The country club may have served up potato salad, too, but there were more forks to wrestle with. These contacts broadened the players' horizons. Gabby Ziegler, the Chicks' captain and morale mainstay, clearly recalls a frigid day when the team was invited to someone's home for a swim. The players wisely declined, leaving their hosts at loose ends, till someone else suggested a round of golf. It was a game Ziegler had no fondness for, but it was the stock invitation, since most of the teams' male supporters spent half their leisure hours on the golf course. To overcome her resistance, a local sports equipment salesman offered to sell Ziegler and her teammates cheap starter sets of clubs. Armed with the right equipment, they soon became converts and hit the links most mornings. ("At least, whenever Johnny Rawlings wasn't mad at us and called a practice," recalls Ziegler. "If we lost a game, he'd say, 'No golf tomorrow.' But I played golf more and more, and later I just got crazy about the game.")

If all this sounds like Norman Rockwell America, that's because it was. The League lasted as long as it did, weathering good times and bad, only by means of solid local support. The team backers toiled ceaselessly to ensure that such support was forthcoming, and that it was merited. They believed in the All-American's founding premises; Wrigley's initial pitch still rang true. Anything that fostered pride was good for the community and good for them. Which is why they meddled and made mistakes, and landed out of their depth in something that had never been tried before.

Each year, weeks or months in advance of the players' arrival, the backers began meeting in the club's offices, usually provided free of charge by the principal hotel. They set the agenda for the welcoming ceremony, wrote the mayor's remarks and decided on a program for the opening game. You can see in their faces, in the stiffly posed photographs that record their contacts with the players, that they took these duties seriously indeed.

Each club had a board, made up of eight or ten men, which hired a business manager and office staff, negotiated with the team manager, made sure the chaperon was in place and the ballpark in order. It would decide whether to increase seating or make it a touch more comfortable, whether to upgrade the dugouts, locker rooms and showers, the scoreboard and the press box. The board members were used to such decisions. They were men of substance, men who had invested their money and time in the All-American's future, men with useful networks of friends and business associates who could be persuaded to lend a hand.

The reasons for their involvement varied. Judge Edward Ruetz, president of the Kenosha Comets for many years, was chiefly concerned with the rising incidence of juvenile delinquency. Nate Harkness, president of the Grand Rapids Chicks, also headed the local Chamber of Commerce, sat on the board of the Kent County Family Service and was a member of half a dozen clubs. J.L. "Hans" Mueller, Fort Wayne's president, oversaw the city's basketball association. None of these men was inclined to sit back and see if the All-American would work. They were determined to make it work, to get their hands dirty if the occasion demanded. One night, in the midst of "a fearsome downpour," Ed Deslauriers and the entire South Bend board rushed to the ballpark, "even those who were dressed in good clothes, grabbed shovels and worked all night digging trenches to drain the water away from the infield," so that the next day's game could take place on schedule.

But the local boosters were human, too. Some, confronted with a troop of young, attractive and seemingly eligible young women, developed a roving eye. One or two club directors—and a couple of managers—were known for their unwelcome gallantries. The League intervened when necessary. Harold Greiner, a Fort Wayne board member, recalls that, in the course of a later season, the club was looking for a new manager, and Hans Mueller enthusiastically volunteered. "Let me put it this way," says Greiner. "Hans fancied himself a lady's man. The players would come to us and say, 'Keep him away from me.' I was forty-two then, but he was up around sixty— too old to be chasing women, even though he didn't get anywhere with them." Greiner's fellow board members quietly vetoed Mueller's offer, appointing in his place the circumspect Greiner.

But that didn't stop the overtures. Tiby Eisen remembers that another, recently widowed, director invited her to a dinner for two. "He told me how lonely he was," she says, "and that he hoped I would stay in town when the season ended, not go back to California. He said he wanted to get to know me better and that something might come of it." Eisen, then in her mid-twenties, was in doubt as to his intentions. "Are you asking me to marry you?" she asked. "Oh, no," said the director, in a shocked tone. "Nothing like that." After this cryptic response, conversation lagged—and to this day, Eisen isn't sure whether he wanted her as a daughter or a girlfriend.

By this time, of course, a team's backers couldn't afford to be side-tracked by infatuation. They were first and foremost businessmen and had their investments to consider. The clubs were non-profit entities, so any contributions were tax-deductible, but no one wanted to be out of pocket for short-falls. The head count after each game was anxiously tallied. Ticket revenues not only kept the clubs afloat, they covered the League's shared costs and the services of Meyerhoff's Management Corporation.

By mid-1945, the teams had relatively few concerns. Fort Wayne and Grand Rapids were doing reasonably well; there would not be a repeat of the previous season's big-city fiasco. In fact, almost three times as many people would pay to see the League play in 1945 as they had in 1943. The future looked secure, and good news arrived from every quarter.

Betsy Jochum, Lou Arnold and Lib Mahon were on the road with the Blue Sox in August when the end of the war was announced. The news came on August 15 when they were in Grand Rapids. All games were canceled and the team traveled overnight to Racine, to a hotel overlooking a park. "God," says Mahon, "at four or five in the morning, people were still out there celebrating in the streets, throwing each other into the fountain. They celebrated all night and all the next day. I was happy myself. I had two brothers in the war."

But when the war ended, one of the League's founding premises went with it. People were no longer asked to support the teams out of patriotism. Instead, the twin themes of family and community came rapidly to the fore—family because reunion was on every returning serviceman's mind, and community because the League cities would enter upon a period of upheaval. And so the All-American shifted focus. Now it would present the players as role models, the game as a sport worth emulating, something that young people could aspire to.

Now the backers turned their attention to juvenile delinquency. Civic administrators looked for ways to keep idle
youngsters occupied. Hence the creation in most League cities
of a Knot Hole Gang, or fan club. Any kid who joined got a
membership card and was entitled to reduced admission on
special nights. Players who appealed to the younger fans,
including Jo Lennard, a "wise-cracking left-fielder" who single-
handedly started a bubble-gum craze among her prepubescent
admirers, were moved front and center in a team's publicity
efforts.

Beginning in 1945, cities began to foster spin-off teams
(composed of both boys and girls) that adopted the All-American's rules. Racine's Junior Girls League would draw over 100
hopefuls to its spring training sessions, and often played a
game at Horlick Field before the scheduled contest.
Muskegon, a 1946 expansion club, would set up a six-team
league that drew 350 kids to the initial tryouts and played
throughout the entire summer. In Kenosha, the Kiwanis Club
sought to "cultivate the young as future fans" by letting them
"pick their favorites, seek autographs and go into huddles for
concerted cheering during the games." In Muskegon, the Opti-
mist Club (whose somewhat exclusive motto was "Friend of the
Boy," although there were co-ed and all-girl Knot Hole Gangs
aplenty) drew 700-odd youngsters to Monday and Saturday
night games.

No wonder, then, that the All-American's code of conduct
rules continued to be enforced. Discipline would not be
relaxed, as Marie Keenan, the League's secretary, rather
ungrammatically made plain in the course of a newsletter: "If
you gals think you're going to get away with wearing slacks
during the post-season series and other times, and other
things that went on, you have another think coming, and it's
going to be quite an expensive experience for you." The players couldn't get a single moment's peace. Having narrowly

survived the war, they were now expected to be idealized, skirted, heavily made-up Big Sisters.

By 1945, girls' baseball was making an impression on the sports world. People argued about whether it was real baseball, but whatever side of the argument they took, no one could deny the players were popular—often more popular than men's teams. *The Baseball Blue Book*, a regular publication that reported baseball statistics for the major leagues, decided to try to figure out why. *Blue Book* publisher Earle Moss chose Fort Wayne, home of the Daisies, for his research project because there were two champion men's teams the Daisies could be compared to.

Fort Wayne's local businesses sponsored a men's professional world champion softball team and a semi-professional baseball team. The men's teams had excellent facilities, played during the day and charged low or no admission. The All-American League team was in its first season, played night games, had temporary bleachers holding a maximum of 3,000 and charged seventy-four cents admission.

Moreover, there was a six-week newspaper strike in Fort Wayne right in the middle of the baseball season. During the strike, the Daisies used word-of-mouth advertising to build their following to average over 1,500 a game, and fan interest grew even more after the strike. The men's pro softball audiences plummeted when there was no newspaper to advertise their games, while the semi-professional men's baseball team won the Indiana state title, playing in Fort Wayne, but the gate for the entire series was under 900.

Moss declared that girls' baseball was not just another version of softball. It was baseball, albeit a form more popular thirty years ago than in 1945. The girls' game drew larger crowds because there was a constant alertness on the playing field, Moss said, and the play contained "spotlighted episodes subordinate to the game contest," such as runners on base constantly poised to steal.

"There were more intentional passes, strike-outs and bases-on-balls and a larger proportion of runners left on bases to runs scored than in standard baseball practice.... It brought about a continual pressure and movement toward the plate—an around-the-diamond threat ... to reach that focal point of game interest," wrote Moss.

The *Blue Book* editor also timed the players, right down to how long it took for a pitch to reach the plate and how long for the average player to make it from home plate to first. Given the game's slightly shorter distances, it took the female players just about the same time as men to make a specific play, he said.

As a final argument in favor of what the girls' game could teach men's baseball, Moss pointed out that the League game "produced more sand-lot activity in this city among both boys and girls, than any influence of the last 25 years."

New figures on the scene for the 1945 season included Fort Wayne's manager, former major-leaguer Bill Wambsganss, who had changed his name to Wamby because it fit better in the box scores. Wamby was distinguished by the fact that he'd made the only unassisted triple play in a World Series game. This story was paraded out with such regularity that even Wamby got thoroughly sick of hearing it. His feat took place in 1920, when he was playing second base for the Cleveland Indians against the Brooklyn Robins. In the fifth inning of the fifth game, there were two Robins on base, who had been given the sign to start running. The batter swung and sent a liner straight to the vigilant Wamby. He caught it, thus making one out. He then touched second, eliminating the runner who'd started for third. The runner who was heading from first to second, transfixed by these developments, stopped dead in his tracks. Wamby calmly walked over and tagged him, completing the triple play.

This was the high point of Wamby's major-league career, but he did reasonably well upon joining the All-American. He spent two seasons at Fort Wayne, followed by another two with the Muskegon Lassies, when they entered the League. He was remembered with affection. Almost every year, his teams stood high in the standings, or lasted in the play-offs until the final game.

In South Bend, Bert Niehoff's replacement as manager was Marty McManus, who had arrived from Kenosha. He was in his early forties, having spent fifteen years in the majors with the St. Louis Browns, the Detroit Tigers and the Boston Red Sox. But his playing days had been over for a decade, and McManus sometimes sought solace in drink.

McManus's arrival coincided with South Bend's decision to expand their board of directors from the customary eight men to a larger, consultative board numbering twenty-five—one of the club's less sensible tinkerings. The Blue Sox president took advantage of the confusion and embarked on a series of unilateral moves, undercutting the manager's authority. Doris Barr, a speed-ball pitcher from Starbuck, Manitoba, who also wielded a good bat, ran into trouble early in the season. McManus decided to shift her to the outfield for a rest. The president, however, insisted that she be put on waivers, and she was picked up by Racine, where she recovered her momentum and helped beat South Bend silly. McManus attempted to reassert his authority by yelling at those players who remained. "He'd just bawl the heck out of girls if they didn't move," says Lucille Moore, the chaperon. "The minute they got a hit, regardless if it was a foul, they had to take off. And if they loafed to first base, there were no words spared." On the road after a game, however, McManus's mood would improve, and he'd tell stories about the good old days.

At one point, the board passed a resolution reaffirming that he had full charge of running the team, but nevertheless continued to meddle. At season's end, McManus resigned and took two years off—only to be lured back in 1948 by the election of an old friend, Dr. Harold Dailey, as club president. His return would prove ill-fated. He continued to drink, his health declined, and he tried to leave again to manage the Springfield Sallies, an expansion team. Dailey dissuaded him from doing so, a decision he lived to regret. "I should have let him go," Dailey later wrote.

Meanwhile, in Grand Rapids, the relocated Chicks were making do with Bernhard "Benny" Meyer. This was his first and only season in the All-American. He had spent four years in the majors as an outfielder, and had extensive experience coaching minor-league men's teams. He freely admitted that he once considered girls' baseball a joke. "But in a few days," he said, "I felt like apologizing to every girl in the League. The entertainment they give the public is nothing less than superb."

Meyer himself was no slouch when it came to mounting a show, but showmanship ran a distant second to the need for victory. He liked to win. His nickname, "Hungry Ben," stemmed from a early-season double-header, in the course of which Meyer sent his best pitcher to the mound in both games against the ailing Blue Sox. A South Bend sportswriter found this a bit much, pointing out that Meyer had four top-notch hurlers to choose from, that the Chicks were in first place and that more than ninety games remained in the schedule. Under these conditions, he wrote, "such hungriness is uncalled for." Meyer disagreed. The previous year (under Max Carey), the Chicks had begun each game with a morale-boosting huddle, during which someone recited an inspiring message. Most of these homilies dealt with such ennobling themes as courage, friendship and faith. When Meyer took over, his pep talk was short and to the point: "Girls, here's what I want to say. If we win this game, I'll give each of you a $5 bill, including the chaperon."

Meyer also liked clowning amiably for the fans. One of his stunts was to bait the umpire. In South Bend, he loved to make life difficult for Gadget Ward, who had quite enough to deal with already. Carey had been on his case about the umpires' personal habits, which included chewing tobacco. Ward received a memo stating that, if they couldn't get through a game without spitting juice all over the field, he was to fire them. As for Meyer, Ward recalls that he "came down on every strike I called. He'd waddle over to home plate, and each time he got there, he'd take his hat off and get right up in my face. Then he'd say, 'You know something, you're the best-dressed umpire in this League. Matter of fact, you're the best umpire in this or any other league.'" After several more compliments, back would go Meyer to the coaching box as fans yelled encouragement, delighted that someone would stand up to the hated official. "The crowd was going wild," says Ward. "But the third time Meyer came over, I called time. I told him, 'Mr. Meyer, I know I'm the best-dressed umpire. I know I'm the best umpire. And I'm going to run your fanny right out of this ballpark the next time you leave that coaching box.' So he put his hat back on and went back to third base."

Despite these diversions, the Chicks could not be inspired. They slid badly in the standings (but managed on one occasion to score a questionable ninth-inning win over Racine, which so appalled Charlie Stis, the Belles' manager, that he attacked the home-plate umpire). Grand Rapids finished the season in third place, a comedown from their championship performance the previous year. Benny Meyer retreated to a men's league, the Chicks found themselves another manager in Johnny Rawlings, and Bill Allington's Rockford Peaches won the championship. The All-Americans headed home again, this time to a brave new post-war future.

1946

⚔

BEDBUGS AND
BEANBALLS

B ack on the Canadian prairies, those players who had
stayed at home had been fascinated for the past three
seasons by the experiences of their friends returning
from the All-American. In 1943, Daisy Knezovich had been
about to marry Dave Junor, so she'd refused the League's initial offer and settled down. But every year, "everyone came
back raving about this glamor League down south, and everybody was having such a good time. I was just busting to go, but
I thought, 'Well, I can't now, I'm married.'" Then the news
came that the League would be holding tryouts in Pascagoula.
"Dave and I talked it over, and he knew I really wanted to go,
and he said, 'Well, you know I could never afford to take you
down there.' So I decided to go."

As for Bonnie Baker, she had promised Maury that she
would quit when he returned from the service: "And my intentions were good. I was going to stay home like a good wife, but
the closer it came to the time to go, the more miserable I got."
Spring training in 1946 was over and the regular season about

to start when Maury looked at her and said, "I know you're not going to be happy here all summer. You might as well go where you're going to be happy." Which Baker very promptly did.

Restrictions on domestic travel had been eased, and the All-American looked forward to a relaxing session in the Deep South. Pascagoula was far from the sleet and snow of the midwest; but spring in Mississippi had its own trials to offer.

Pascagoula was an abandoned air base, located on the Gulf of Mexico just west of the Alabama state line. Dr. Harold Dailey, the avid chronicler of South Bend's woes, vilified the site as "the worst mess I ever saw. The housing conditions were terrible. They were war-built barracks used by the shipyard workers. They were alive with roaches and bugs of all kinds. The main field was rutted and the smaller diamonds were unmown grass. We got the diamonds repaired, and they tried to build extra diamonds that were finished about the time we were through."

The players of the Glamor League coped as best they could. Jean Faut recalls that "we bought that place out of DDT. You'd sprinkle it across the doorway, or the bugs would march right in." Daisy Junor was filled with a mixture of horror and admiration: "The cockroaches were so big, they didn't scurry, they strolled." Connie Wisniewski shared Junor's sentiments: "You could have put saddles on 'em." People kept the lights on and their suitcases firmly closed. Betty Tucker, a novice pitcher, lost no opportunity to turn the situation to training advantage. "We'd get oranges for lunch," she says, "and instead of eating them, we'd take them back with us, and if we saw a cockroach on the wall, we'd whip the orange at it."

At least this remote starting point gave teams a chance to play outdoors every day during spring training. There were also a series of games en route back north, through what Dailey called "bad mountain country on long night jumps." The idea here was to expose the All-American to other centers, to attract new recruits. In 1946, the clubs played twenty-seven cities in eleven states. It was in fact a good investment—spearheaded by Meyerhoff—in publicity and recruiting, but a somewhat cost-intensive one. Most of the proceeds went to local charities, including the Colored Orphans and Industrial Home of Lexington, Kentucky, which benefitted to the tune of $300. The clubs, who had to contribute to the cost of these games, thought them a waste of time. Meyerhoff disagreed. It was the way to enlarge the talent pool, to attract attention. Very few prospective recruits had the ability to attend spring training on their own. The League had to go to them. Sometimes a player would be spotted in the pre-game tryouts and sent directly to Chicago for assignment to a team. More commonly, they were invited to spring training the following year.

In 1946, the League elected once more to shrink the ball, this time to eleven inches. The previous year, after a wave of no-hit, no-run games that led the organizers to conclude that pitchers were too much in control, the pitching distance had been increased by two feet. Not content with these modifications, the All-American then decided to move away from softball's underhand pitch. In 1946, it allowed for the first time a modified sidearm delivery. Suddenly, the pitcher's repertoire was increased. She could develop a fastball, a curve or a sinker. This was an interim measure that would lead two seasons later to an exclusively overhand throw.

The press reported public reaction. "There are two schools of thought on the subject," said Dick Day, the sports editor of the Rockford *Register-Republic.* "One group contends that the girls' League is ready now to make a clean break with the past, discard the traditional underhand pitch of softball entirely and adopt overhand or sidearm delivery. Others take an exact opposite view. They hold to the theory that overhand pitching of steady quality is a virtual impossibility with women, and that the fans don't want it."

Day's comments stemmed from an interview he'd held in Pascagoula with Johnny Gottselig. "Back in 1943, when this League was formed," Gotsellig told him, "pitching was no problem. Amateur softball leagues had an abundance of good twirlers eager to turn pro. But times have changed. The League has advanced to the stage where not many stars from the softball ranks can move right in with the regulars. There just aren't enough top-flight pitchers in softball ranks to meet our requirements anymore." This shortage had not escaped the notice of Gottselig's protégée, Bonnie Baker. In between persuading Maury that her future lay with the All-American, she had touched base with her former manager in Regina: "I asked him, 'Where are all the softball players? I can remember when they used to be falling off the end of the bench.' He told me that he was having to steal players from other teams."

But it was the same story everywhere. Tiby Eisen had found the previous winter that softball was no longer the sport of choice in Los Angeles; the decline in softball's popularity had begun. Now that the war was over, there were far more interesting things for people to do; they certainly didn't start to play sandlot baseball. The softball leagues had been the All-American's farm system. But the more that Meyerhoff and Carey shifted the rules of play toward baseball, the longer it took to train a recruit, who might or might not succeed. If she didn't, there was nowhere for her to go. A club couldn't send its rookies down to the minors for a bit more experience. It was do or die, in front of everyone. But the All-American pressed ahead anyway. The real question—where were all the sidearm or overhand pitchers going to come from, given that there weren't enough underhanders to go around?—was shuffled aside.

Most of the League's pitchers attempted to adapt. Throwing the smaller ball with a sidearm motion increased their speed, but it forced them to use their bodies in a different way. Jean Faut, who pitched for South Bend, didn't like the sidearm at first, but with a strong arm and a good curve, she held her own. Umpire Gadget Ward one day challenged her during batting practice. "I can't understand why these girls can't hit you," he said. "I can hit you." Faut accepted his challenge and took the mound. Ward grabbed a bat, stepped into the box and succeeded only in embarrassing himself for five minutes straight. "Afterward," said Faut, "he still couldn't understand why he couldn't hit me."

But Faut was an extraordinary pitcher, one of the All-American's best. Other pitchers, including Janet Perkins, couldn't handle even the modified sidearm. She had been drafted by the Kenosha Comets, but 1946 was her first and final year. She wasn't all that happy. The punishing whirlwind of baseball and travel, more baseball and more travel, didn't leave much time for a personal life. "I wasn't going to wreck my arm," she says, "'cause I knew I wasn't going to be there that long." Perkins packed it in and returned to Saskatchewan. Nor was Perkins alone. Carolyn Morris, a beautiful woman from Arizona with an outstanding windmill delivery, pitched her last game in 1946. Rather than imperil her throwing arm, she returned to the sunbelt softball leagues.

Others saw the sidearm as a hurdle to be overcome. Joanne Winter, a player since 1943, had enjoyed only modest success, losing as many games as she won. She'd had very little in the way of formal training, having picked up her skills from watching other players. "I often wonder what I really looked like," she says. "I put all kinds of stuff on the ball—I invented my own way of turning it—but I wasn't sophisticated or good enough, and struggled along." After the 1944 season, she had confided her unhappiness to the man who'd encouraged her—her father. She wrote him, saying that she might not be cut out for pitching duties.

Her father disagreed and sent her in the off-season to a well-known pitcher in Phoenix, Arizona, named Kuhn Rosen.

To her surprise, Winter found that he favored the wrist-ball style she'd seen practiced by Canadian Nicky Fox (the former Helen Nicol), who threw for Kenosha. "And Nicky was absolutely tremendous. She could make it take off—she had a great rise ball. So I thought, 'Well, maybe I can do that, too.' And I tried it, but it didn't fit me." In fact, Winter sank during 1945 to an all-time low, losing twenty-two games (eleven of them by a single run) and winning only seven.

But Winter persisted. She returned to Phoenix, this time to the tutelage of Knolly Trujillo, who favored a slingshot delivery—an underhand throw with minimal windup. Trujillo worked at the local fire department, and Winter went down there every day and pitched, while her father watched. "I took a look at what Trujillo had, and I thought, 'This is neat,' so I changed to a slingshot. That fit me, just half of a windmill. By golly, I remember the first time I made that thing hop, and the catcher said, 'That's it!' So now I had something different. It was so different that when I went back to the League, I turned myself around." Winter would tie with Connie Wisniewski in 1946 for the all-time League season record of thirty-three wins.

Other changes were afoot. In 1946, the League expanded to include the Muskegon Lassies, managed by Ralph "Buzz" Boyle, and the Peoria Redwings, who started off under the direction of Bill "Raw Meat" Rodgers. Rodgers was hastily replaced by Johnny Gottselig, who would eventually manage four teams in the All-American.

Muskegon was an industrial and shipping center, with a population of roughly 45,000, but it had an excellent ballpark called Marsh Field, which the Lassies shared with the city's Triple-A men's team. Peoria, Illinois' second-largest city, was something else again. A *Saturday Evening Post* article commented on its contradictions: "An abundance of churches and an abundance of saloons, a highly-developed civic consciousness and a long and odorous history of gambling and sin dens."

Bumper corn crops from the surrounding countryside had long been parlayed into a brisk distilling business. Peoria produced more hard liquor than any other American city. Nor had Prohibition fazed it unduly. Other industries helped it weather the dry spell, and when booze was legalized again, the distilleries picked up steam. As a result, it contained several wealthy areas, located on high bluffs overlooking the Illinois River—the home of such personalities as Faye Dancer's admiring mobster.

With two new centers in the League, two new teams had to be created. But with the difficulties in recruiting new players starting to mount, clubs once more looked to allocation as the best source of good players.

Pepper Paire was one of the first to be moved in 1946. She interpreted her trade as a plan to plunder the powerful Fort Wayne Daisies, who had nearly won the championship their first year out. Paire liked Fort Wayne, and didn't want to be traded: "I had been with the team for two years [counting its incarnation as the Minneapolis Millerettes]. We felt we were going to win everything this time out." But it was not to be.

The Rockford Peaches were due to see their ranks depleted as well. Dick Day reported from Pascagoula that a rival club's director had told him, "Well, we certainly have got to break up the Peaches ... they're too strong for the rest of the League." And, sure enough, Bill Allington saw two of his most experienced players snatched away.

Some players, as usual, were bewildered and hurt. They looked for hidden motives in their trades. One claims to have been shuffled off the week after she ran into her manager at a secluded restaurant in the company of a woman who was not his wife. For the most part, though, it was simply Carey and Meyerhoff playing mix-and-match to maintain something resembling equal strength, to make sure that no one club remained perpetually on top or languished forever in the doldrums.

Nor was the Chicago League inactive. It continued to lure malcontent All-Americans with inflated salary offers, forcing Carey and Meyerhoff to attempt a truce. In 1946, they reached a verbal agreement with the Chicago owners, pledging not to raid each other's players but agreeing that any player released by one league was fair game for the other. Meyerhoff knew it wouldn't last. "The stronger the Chicago League becomes," he wrote, "the more of a threat they are. The working agreement wouldn't last a minute if they thought they could get our girls. It is only because we occupy a stronger position that they are interested in an agreement at all."

What was the All-American's allegedly stronger position? Setting aside salaries, the All-American was a classier act. With Wrigley at the helm, players had traveled in extreme comfort. They stayed in quality hotels and were featured in national magazines. Household names came to see them play. The All-American may have been finding it difficult to resolve its problems, but it was still "the glamor loop" to its players.

The season began, amid the customary rash of injuries. Every spring, pulled tendons and broken bones plunged effective teams into a tailspin that depressed both players and fans and set the club directors off in anxious pursuit of suitable replacements. Given the chronic shortage of new blood, a lot of the All-Americans played hurt. Their mishaps were standard issue—broken fingers for the catcher, ankle sprains, spike wounds and torn knee ligaments for the runners. Experienced managers became skilled at stop-gap measures. During one game, Dottie Ferguson jarred her leg while sliding home. Within minutes, her foot and ankle began to swell. "So Bill Allington took me into the clubhouse and told the groundskeeper to get a pail of hot water and another of ice water," she says. "He dipped my foot first in one, then in the other. Then he told me to put my shoe back on and run on the track. I did, and the next day I played ball."

Catchers were vulnerable. Pepper Paire broke a finger when a foul tip hit her in the course of an exhibition game. The doctor applied an enormous "bird cage" splint, but Johnny Rawlings exchanged it for a couple of popsicle sticks the following day. "We opened against South Bend," she says, "and they'd heard I was hurt, but it just looked like I had a band aid on. They kept passing by me on the bench, saying, 'Hear you've been hurt.' I'd just say, 'Naw, it's nothing.' They had a lot of fast runners—Bonnie Baker, Senaida "Shoo Shoo" Wirth and Charlene "Shorty" Pryer. They were all set to run against me," knowing that, with her finger taped straight out, the ball she threw would probably sail into the outfield. "Bonnie got on base first and took off for second. To this day I don't know how I did it, but I threw her out. Next up was Wirth, and it was the same thing all over again. Of course, it was painful. All year it was painful. That's why today I can point three ways at once."

Later, in the midst of a crucial play-off, Paire twisted her ankle and played the final seven games with her foot taped and frozen: "I had to wear my coach's shoe, that's how bad it was swollen." As for Bonnie Baker, she was knocked unconscious for ten minutes as a result of falling into the dugout in pursuit of a foul ball, then had her hand broken not once but twice when struck by a batter. Both times she was called for interference. The first time put her out for the rest of the season. The second was only a hairline fracture, and she continued to catch with her hand taped and the mitt packed with extra sponge padding. By season's end, the fracture had become a full-fledged break.

The head injuries were the most frightening. Dorothy Hunter's first and only season as a player was notable for a brushback from Olive Bend Little (her best friend, but that didn't count in the heat of combat). "It was the first time she pitched against me," says Hunter, "but she knew very well I was a sucker for a high inside ball. She got me right in the side of the face and I went down like a ton of bricks. It knocked me silly and I was in tears, but I got to first base." Little was so shaken by the incident that she walked the next three batters, giving Hunter a walk home.

Sometimes, of course, the brushbacks were intentional—a matter of retaliation. Dolly Tesseine, who played with both the Lassies and Chicks, explains, "We played a pretty rough game. I was at shortstop when Gabby Ziegler spiked me coming into second. Ziggy was about as aggressive a player as there was. I said to her, 'Next time you do that, I'm going to jam the ball down your throat.' When I came to bat, she threw at my head—Ziggy was a pitcher then. She put me on the ground. But when she came up, our pitcher fired for her head. Nobody got hurt, and that was that."

And no apologies, either—but excitement usually over-ruled remorse. Once, Dottie Ferguson, at second base, took a throw from the shortstop, looked around and saw that a runner was coming in from first standing up. "I stepped on the bag and started to throw to first for a double play. I figured that the gal would duck, but she didn't, and I got her right in the forehead. It didn't knock her out for very long, and I thought, 'Well, I couldn't have had much on that throw.' Isn't that awful? But you didn't go into base standing up unless you were asking to be killed."

The All-American's famous "strawberries" were unique. Players went into battle with twenty inches of unprotected flesh between knee and upper thigh. In theory, runners ought to sink into their slides at the last moment, avoiding a long and painful scrape along the ground. Actually, they slid in whatever way the situation demanded. Basepaths were supposed to be sand, but after a couple of innings they were down to hard, unyielding dirt—or, in some cases, cinder. As a result, the most aggressive runners spent all season with one or both legs a mass of wounds that never had time to mend or scab over. The League provided them with sliding pads—bulky efforts rather like surgical dressings that were supposed to be taped to their legs. But these kept coming off. Besides, players thought they looked disconcertingly like a Kotex pad hanging down from under their skirts. Several chaperons experimented with makeshift remedies, including "doughnuts" made from rolled-up towels, but these too came unstuck almost immediately, and looked even worse. No wonder that players returned home covered with scar tissue. No wonder that the managers couldn't bear to watch them slide. Playing in the All-American qualified its players for the Purple Heart.

In what little leisure time they had available, the players' enthusiasms were typical. Music was big, with allegiance split between Frank Sinatra and Bing Crosby. Tiby Eisen spent time experimenting with novel hairdos; her teammates could count on a free home permanent. She was also adept at jitterbugging and liked to enter competitions in the off-season. Dottie Kamenshek was a crossword-puzzle addict. The wild-at-heart Faye Dancer waited eagerly for the newest Tarzan movie starring Johnny Weismuller. These were the pastimes that fans could read about in their local papers.

Other hobbies were not so well-publicized. Many players liked to gamble. Poker was the card game of choice, although the aisle of a bus on an overnight trip was the perfect venue for craps. In the hotel room after bed check, players would bring out the cards, and money changed hands until dawn broke. Bonnie Baker was a dab hand at poker. She dealt the cards at every turn, with such other card-sharks as Lib Mahon, Lil Faralla, Twi Shively and Ruth Williams. Daisy Junor played, too, but always heeded Baker's warning when the stakes got rarefied: "She'd say, 'Get out,' and I did. She could clean their clocks in no time," Junor remembers. Lou Arnold, who didn't play, says of Baker: "She used to come on that bus, looking like a movie star, and she'd sit there with a Coke in one hand and her cards in the other and the sweat would be coming down her face."

The Coke bottle became Baker's trademark. "I drank twenty-four bottles a day," she says. "Hot, cold, lukewarm, whatever. I went to bed with one on my night table and got up in the morning and drank it." So pressing was this addiction that Chet Grant, the Blue Sox' newly appointed manager, allowed her to bring a supply into the dugout, in flagrant violation of the rules.

Baker had competition on the card-shark circuit. In Grand Rapids, Mildred Earp led a hard-core group of poker fanatics. Dottie Hunter, the chaperon, saw this as a disruptive trend: "The kids would get paid and then lose a whole cheque in a game. So one of them was stupid enough to come to me and say, 'Gee, Dottie, I don't have any money. Could you loan me some?' So I asked what happened, and she told me she'd lost it all in a card game. That did it right there. I cut out all poker games, on the road, anyway. What they did at home I don't know, but nobody ever came and told me they lost their money after that. But these young kids could be talked into anything, you know, so you had to watch them like a hawk."

Many players, making real wages for the first time in their lives, had difficulty sticking to a budget. One young Rockford Peach was chronically short of funds, and chaperon Millie Lundahl was forced to act. She persuaded the board to withhold half the player's salary until the end of the season. The player protested bitterly—at first. "At the end of the season," says Lundahl, "she came and apologized. She said she would never have saved it. She said she was sorry that she'd given me a hard time."

Other chaperons considered gambling the least of several evils the young women were capable of. At least it kept players in the hotel and out of trouble. The managers had their own prohibited pleasure—illicit slot machines that Fred Leo remembers were a staple of Elks Clubs in every city. However, anything that smacked of wagering on the games themselves was not tolerated. Hunter recalls that Johnny Rawlings was particularly firm on this point: "He took his job very seriously, and all these professional baseball men, they knew all the ins and outs about betting. He was from that era of the White Sox scandal [when Shoeless Joe Jackson and his teammates conspired with gamblers to throw the World Series]. He'd get mad because the fans would come to some of the ball players and ask 'Who's goin' to pitch tonight?' He didn't want them to tell anybody anything because he thought these guys were goin' to bet. He'd seen a lot of betting in the big leagues and he didn't believe in it."

Road trips were the time for vigilance from manager and chaperon, but it could be a rough game of cat-and-mouse for the caretakers. One night in Fort Wayne, Allington sat in the Hotel Van Orman lobby until four a.m. waiting to confront players who had dared to stay out past curfew—in this case, they included Harrell and Kamenshek. Allington didn't find out until the next day that the players had been in their rooms well before the allotted time. They had made their way in via the fire escape, simply to vex him. Sometimes, a chaperon hoped that her players would go out on the town rather than rampage through their accommodations. Lib Mahon recalls a handful of bad apples who ran up and down the hallways "throwing beer labels on the ceiling so they'd stick." But this, says Mahon, was the exception: "You could count those people on one hand." Their behavior, coupled with the stealthy practice of obtaining more than the regulation two beers each by having non-drinkers order for them, was about as far as the All-Americans went in terms of depravity.

There were, not surprisingly, ceaseless violations of the anti-fraternizing rule that prohibited players from opposing teams—many of whom were former teammates, due to the allocation merry-go-round—from spending leisure time together. This edict covered "room parties, auto trips to out-of-the-way eating places, et cetera. However, friendly discussions in lobbies are permissible." On the surface, it had some validity—"to sustain the complete spirit of rivalry between clubs." But it was the underlying fear that prompted the League to levy stiff fines for violations—the fear of lesbianism. The League sometimes moved players around to break up a suspected romance, and there was no point unless it was followed up by a strict rule that kept them from continuing to see each other. But after four seasons of play, some players had quite a roster of friends on other teams. And because many players returned to their home towns right after the end of the season, there wasn't much chance to socialize if you didn't grab it when you were on the road. The rule only succeeded in further restricting a player's social life.

It wasn't too difficult a regulation for prying officials to monitor and make a show of enforcing. Nicky Fox remembers taking the streetcar from Kenosha to nearby Racine, where her friends Sophie Kurys and Maddy English lived and played. The three young women spent the day on the waterfront. Then it was time for Fox to head back to Kenosha, meet the rest of the Comets and return to Racine to play the Belles that evening. "So I took the electric streetcar back," she says. "When it got to the outskirts of Kenosha, it ran into a picket line. J.I. Case Implements were on strike, and they'd taken a propane tube and laid it across the tracks. We sat there so long I could have walked home, but I stayed on the streetcar, and got to the station just in time to meet the rest of the team. There was no mystery about where I'd been; the streetcar only went to Racine. So there it was—fraternizing. I had to go home and get my uniform and catch the next streetcar back, and they fined me $25."

And players continued their bouts with managers. In South Bend, Marty McManus had taken his leave and was replaced by Chet Grant, a former football player. Bonnie Baker didn't always see eye to eye with Grant, who was known for his sarcastic turn of phrase. One Sunday afternoon, during batting practice, his remarks put Baker's back up. "Whatever he said, it just hit me the wrong way," she says, "so I just went into the clubhouse and sat there." Maury was in town, and she told him that it was time to go back to Saskatchewan. "Think about it," Maury advised. "Don't do anything you'll be sorry for." Maury then proposed a deal: "You go to the ballpark, get in your uniform and go out on the field. If he doesn't have you in the lineup, I'll take you home." Baker did so. Grant had forgotten the incident, and Baker played the double-header as scheduled.

Meanwhile, in Rockford, relations between Allington and the Peaches were plumbing new depths. He rode the rookies hard, while veterans like Harrell and Kamenshek tried to calm them down by promising revenge. Their retaliation was poetic justice. Allington was in the habit of watching batting practice from the third-base coaching box. Kamenshek, whose hitting had improved under his tutelage, knocked sharp line drives straight at him. "We'd make him skip rope," she says. When it came his turn, Allington would respond with the meanest grounders he could muster, but thanks once again to his skilled instruction, the team was ready for them.

In Grand Rapids, Pepper Paire was making life hard for Johnny Rawlings. She had discovered that he had a stomach ulcer. "I was in a hitting slump for a while," she says. "I kept popping up, so Rawlings would tell me, 'Get your elbows out. Get your elbows out.' I got sick and tired of hearing this, so I went out to the plate and stuck my elbows way out, up around my ears. Dottie Hunter told me later that Rawlings was so mad he went back into the locker room and threw up." This wasn't the only time that Pepper ignored Rawlings' instructions. The cautious Rawlings instructed her to take intentional walks in a game against Rockford, whose pitchers feared her post-slump hitting power. She drew three in a row, but each time, the next batter had struck out to end the inning. Intentional walks involve a pitch-out, thrown well beyond the batter's reach—but Paire had kept her eye on the pitcher's technique, and saw that the tosses were close enough to get a bat on: "She threw one just outside the plate, so I reached out and popped it into the right field stands and we won the game. Rockford was standing there half asleep. If they'd been alert, someone could have caught it, but I got them off-guard." Rawlings was happy, and even Allington, whose team she'd just defeated, came trotting over for a congratulatory handshake.

And so the 1946 season unwound, marked like all the others by endless hours on the bus—long hauls around Lake Michigan and through the rolling farmlands of Wisconsin and Illinois. "We'd get on at midnight and pull into town at seven o'clock the next morning," says Hunter. "The players would fall into bed and I'd have to get them up to make sure they got to the game on time that night. That was a grueling schedule, I don't care what anybody says. But they were young enough to take it and survive."

The team bus—cramped, with low ceilings and overhead shelves packed full of blankets and pillows, rows of two seats along one side and singles on the other—doubled as hotel and locker room. Some buses had no toilet, which meant that a ride was punctuated with roadside stops. Incredibly, regulations decreed that a player struggle into a skirt—at two in the morning, in the middle of nowhere—before she could get off and walk to the gas station restroom. If the bus stopped in a town, the local all-night hangers-on would gather like flies.

The Fort Wayne Daisies' bus was a tight ship. When Harold Greiner managed the team, he would disembark first, making sure the coast was clear, keeping an eye out for unwanted

Romeos. "Once," he says, "there were some men in the street, and some smart aleck said something. I didn't hear what it was; they'd watched till I wasn't nearby. Anyway, all of a sudden I hear 'Wow!' I turned around and saw that June Peppas had decked the guy—and I mean she really decked him. He crawled away."

The Grand Rapids Chicks' bus, on the other hand, was noted for that old-time religion, as interpreted by Pepper Paire and Alma Ziegler: "Especially if it was on a Sunday, Zig and I would deliver a 'Sermon on the Mound.' We'd put our jackets and caps on backwards and have a little holy gospel. We'd get the rookies down on their knees in the aisle, and ask them, 'Are you truly in the game? Are you going to get a hit tomorrow? Say Hallelujah, brother! Hallelujah, brother.' I think I missed my calling."

And when they weren't receiving the good word from Pepper, they sang. Dottie Green played harmonica aboard the Rockford bus, while Millie Lundahl led a chorus of "I've Been Working on the Railroad" or "Till We Meet Again." Bill Allington sat quietly and listened—a song was the only thing that kept him off his customary post mortem—but Harold Greiner was often persuaded to provide the Daisies with a lullaby. "I'd be thinking about dozing off, when one of the gals would say, 'Okay, boss, it's time to put us to sleep.' I'd have to sing some songs then. I used to have a good voice. I didn't sing any boogie-woogie stuff, but one song they liked was 'The Best Things in Life Are Free.' Oh, I had about twenty that I could sing, and pretty soon, you wouldn't hear a peep out of them."

Sophie Kurys, the Racine Belles' champion base-stealer, remembers the last play-off game of the 1946 season with pleasure, and everyone who saw it agrees. Her club had topped the standings and had beaten the Blue Sox 3-2 in seventeen innings to win the semi-final. Meanwhile, Allington's Peaches had triumphed over Connie Wisniewski and the Chicks. The Belles and Peaches met for the championship, which came down to a final and deciding match.

"We had drawn almost 7,000 people to Horlick Field," Kurys remembers. "It didn't have any fences in the outfield, but people had pulled their cars back there, like at a drive-in. They were standing on the roofs to get a better view. It was the most exciting game I ever participated in. It was only a 1-0 score, but there was so much hitting, so much action. We were standing on our heads out there, doing everything to catch the ball."

Kurys is modest; she won the game herself. Joanne Winter pitched for Racine, giving up thirteen hits over fourteen innings and stranding nineteen runners on base. "She got the hard hitters out and walked the easy ones," says Kurys. Meanwhile, Carolyn Morris, throwing for the Peaches, pitched a no-hit game for nine innings. In the scoreless tenth, the Belles got two runners on base, and Allington pulled her in favor of Millie Deegan. This was acknowledged to be the turning point. Deegan, a former outfielder, was less adept at holding runners on base. In the fourteenth, Kurys hit a single, stole second and came sliding home to score on a single by Betty Trezza. Max Carey, who witnessed the contest, was later quoted as saying that it was the finest game he'd ever seen, even in the majors. Carey was always good for a quote, but this time he was right.

And so, at the close of 1946, club directors totaled the season's gate. There was good news and bad. South Bend drew 113,000 people; Grand Rapids even more. Muskegon, with a population of 80,000, sold an astounding 140,000 tickets. But attendance at Rockford and Fort Wayne declined compared with the previous year. Meyerhoff and Carey seemed oblivious; they were delighted with the teams that were doing well. Expansion was unfolding as it should, and the money was rolling in.

Interest in girls' baseball seemed to be growing beyond the midwest. During the winter of 1946, Meyerhoff was forced to scotch rumors that Mexican promoters were poised to raid the All-American, offering a wide variety of inducements, including higher salaries, to relocate south of the border. This story (which had a grain of truth) was broken by the Fort Wayne newspaper, and Meyerhoff wrote an open letter to ease the minds of fans who feared they would lose their favorites. It was true, he said, that the League's salaries couldn't match what the Mexicans were offering. And the All-American scouting system "consisted of one man," the widely traveled Gottselig. Nonetheless, Meyerhoff doubted that the All-Americans would be permitted to go abroad by their husbands, boyfriends and families. Nor would money be a deciding factor. "Most of the girls," he said, would stay put. They had, after all signed up to play "for Coca-Colas and glory."

1947

OUR GIRLS IN HAVANA

After the steamy, insect-ridden experience of Pascagoula, spring training in 1947 was pure glamor. That year, Meyerhoff shipped 170 players—rookies and veterans alike—to Havana, Cuba. Coincidentally, the Brooklyn Dodgers had already been there that winter, in search of peace and quiet. They had feared that to train as usual in the southern states might mean trouble for their latest recruit, an infielder named Jackie Robinson. Meyerhoff, however, wanted more publicity, not less. He got it. And All-American players like to remind people that they, not the big-league Dodgers, drew the larger crowds to the *Gran Stadium de Havana*.

The Cubans were baseball mad. One of their home-town favorites was Fidel Castro, a promising pitcher with his university team. The youthful law student had previously been scouted by at least two major-league clubs, but turned down an offer (complete with $5,000 signing bonus) from the New York Giants, explaining that he liked being an amateur and wanted to complete his studies—thus leaving North Americans to ponder one of the more intriguing "what ifs" of modern history.

Prior to their departure, Max Carey had dusted off his thesaurus and published a glowing description of the typical

All-American player: "A professional ballplayer knows the answer to not only baseball—but because she has kept her eyes and ears open, she has become travel-wise and experienced and knows how to deport herself in any company—being unselfish, modest, humble, without braggadocio, cooperative, non-primadonnaish, winning graciously, losing sportingly—taking hard knocks as a matter of course and blaming none for her mistakes or her shortcomings."

The All-American players were billeted at the Seville-Biltmore Hotel, from which they were bused to practices at the stadium or the university campus. The turbulence that would soon explode in rebellion against the regime of Cuba's president, Fulgencio Batista, was very close to the surface, but the players did not immediately discern it. Their first impressions were those of all first-time travelers from a wealthy country, dropped suddenly and unexpectedly (the majority had never been outside North America) into the Third World. Hair-raising traffic struck them as the clearest and most present danger. "Bus drivers would scare the daylights out of us," says Lucille Moore, the South Bend chaperon. "We'd start down these tiny narrow streets, and they'd never take their hands off the horn." A hard day's practice simply wasn't possible beneath the intense Caribbean sun. Training sessions took place in the morning or at night, leaving the days free for closely chaperoned sight-seeing expeditions.

Dorothy Schroeder remembers the contrasts. "What struck me about those places was that you were either rich or poor. There was no in-between. Even in Havana, when we rode the bus to the ball park, we went through neighborhoods that were plush, and then maybe two blocks down the street the little kids were playing out in the street. From toddler age to maybe seven or eight, all they wore was a T-shirt. It was an education, it really was."

Food very quickly became the prime topic of conversation and focus of discontent. Breakfast and supper were served barracks-style in the hotel or at local restaurants, at the League's expense. Many players found the food unappetizing. It included greasy eggs and alligator steak. One of Moore's charges, Daisy Junor, "used to send things back constantly. She sent some pancakes back one morning because they were too hard. When they brought some more, she stuck her fork in them and they squirted at her." A meal allowance was supposed to cover lunch, but restaurant prices, especially for American-style cooking, were high. As a result, the players ended up at a bar named Sloppy Joe's, which they'd heard, erroneously, had been made famous by Ernest Hemingway. Dorothy Schroeder expected it to be world-class, but, not surprisingly, she was disappointed to find "it was just like an ordinary bar anywhere." At least it served hamburgers and sandwiches, which the players supplemented with coconuts filled with ice cream and half-pineapples (a nickel each) that they could buy in the street.

Ordinary tourists might cope with unpalatable food, but baseball players needed to keep their strength up. The All-Americans wanted something done, and Joanne Winter, then in her fifth year with the Racine Belles, was appointed the unwilling leader of a mini-revolt. A hungry group of malcontents gathered on the hotel roof and bolstered their courage by knocking back the local *cerveza*. Winter was appointed spokesperson, and found herself the next day facing Meyerhoff, Max Carey and "whoever else was down there—all the League guys and managers. I'm thinking, 'I guess this is the end for me.' And then I thought, 'To heck with it. It's not right.' So I told them, 'You have over a hundred girls here, and you're expecting us to kill ourselves on a ball field, practice and play every day for almost a month, and you're trying to say you can feed this army on stuff we can't eat? The orange juice tastes like castor oil.'" To Winter's relief, Meyerhoff accepted the criticism and coughed up an additional daily meal allowance. Multiplied by 170 players and the three weeks remaining in Havana, this dramatically inflated spring training's final cost. Money was becoming a sore point between the clubs and League officials, whom individual teams would accuse of high living on foreign shores and capitulation to cosseted hired help. But the clubs were wrong. Havana was cheap compared to other training venues. The entire trip, even counting air fare, cost less than had Pascagoula, or would Opa-Locka, Florida, the following year.

By all accounts, opening night at the *Gran Stadium de Havana* was something to behold. The weather was perfect, with a cooling breeze off the Gulf of Mexico. More than 15,000 fans jammed their way through the turnstiles—the largest crowd to ever see a girls' baseball game. As many more would witness the three subsequent contests. The Cubans began by pointing and whistling at the unfamiliar sight, but soon grew more enthusiastic, cheering every play.

The All-Americans quickly became used to the aggressive interest of Latin American men, who welcomed the young and more liberated North Americans. Players were warned not to venture out alone. If they got on a public bus, they'd be pinched. Kissing noises followed them down the street. "But there was something about the atmosphere down there," Moore admits. "It just made you feel that you'd like to skip and dance."

Or hire a translator. Fortunately (or not, depending on your point of view), a couple of the players spoke Spanish—a fact they kept from their hosts. One of them, Marge Villa, provided a running translation of many encounters. Dorothy Schroeder and her teammates (several of whom were blonde) were taken on a factory tour. "People down there are all dark-eyed and dark-haired. When they see a blonde, you better watch out. So we were in the factory, and Marge was with us. The workers were making comments about the '*gringas*,' and she understood it all. When we got back to the hotel, she told us they were saying things like 'Look at the rear end on that one,' and then they'd smile and we thought they were being real nice."

The players also received a crash course in Cuban politics. Spring training ran through May 1, International Workers' Day, a traditional excuse for a boisterous parade. In 1947 Cuba, however, the occasion provided a focus for growing anti-Batista sentiment. On May Day eve, military authorities advised the League to keep its people indoors, and the players were issued emergency rations.

As it turned out, the Saville-Biltmore made an excellent vantage point for the parade. Players were able to augment their food supply by lowering baskets of money to the street vendors below (some of it disappeared). On the rooftop, where many players gathered to watch, they could see the rooftops opposite, guarded by soldiers with machine guns.

May Day passed without serious incident, but the players' presence in the hotel made for a spectacle all its own. Cuban men lurked lewdly around, hoping to catch a glimpse of them. Daisy Junor retains a memory of admirers "in white Panama suits, who'd sit in little alcoves across the street, masturbating and watching us. Then the police would come with their billy clubs. They'd bang them on the cement and the guys would scatter. But after the police left, they'd be back. We went down to the front desk to report them, and the hotel staff told us, 'Well, don't look.'"

The League had decided that Havana's vibrant nightclub scene was strictly off-limits. Indeed, venturing out after dark was frowned upon, except when heavily chaperoned. This did not deter the unsinkable Faye Dancer, who managed to find her way to a cemetery, where the practice was to exhume corpses after the coffins disintegrated. Dancer—a blonde— amazed her teammates by launching into an "Alas, Poor Yorick" soliloquy, addressed to a handy skull. But Dancer was not alone in bending the rules. Betty Tucker and several daring cohorts decided to accept an invitation from two university students who'd come to watch them practice: "They were really good-lookin' fellas. They said they'd take us around and show us some of the sights. So we thought, 'There's two of them and four of us. That's okay.'"

The illicit date can best be described as Andy Hardy's Sisters Meet Casanova's Illegitimate Sons. At one point on the tour of Havana hot spots, they were approached by a man "with an itty-bitty mustache." One of the students warned them against such men. "They're all gigolos," he said. But, as the evening wore on, with an even seedier club on the agenda, the players were unnerved to find that they were now being squired by four young men, one of whom sported that very sort of mustache.

Things looked darker still when the students suggested splitting up into two cars. "Well," says Tucker, "we went to this next club, a little downstairs place, and I said, 'Be sure if we have a drink it's just Coca-Cola in a bottle, so they can't put anything in it.' Then we were dancing for a while, and Maggie [the bilingual Marge Villa] comes over and says, 'This guy is terrible. He's kissing me on the neck.' And I say, 'Mine's singing.' So we told them we had to get back for curfew. They asked us out for the following night, and Maggie didn't want to, but I thought if we refused, they might not take us back to the hotel. So I said, 'Sure, fine,' and meanwhile I'm winking at Maggie, and one of the guys is asking me why I'm making faces, and I tell him I have a nervous condition. We laughed about it a lot, but we swore we'd never do that again."

The 1947 season was distinguished by the absence of Bill Allington, who remained in California, unable to get time off from his job at Twentieth-Century Fox. This suited Dorothy Harrell, who had decided that she "couldn't stand listening to him." Now she settled in to cope with two interim managers,

Bill Edwards and Eddie Ainsmith, whose combined efforts would produce a sixth-place showing for the team.

Those players who could abide Allington's presence yearned for his return. The only thing that Edwards and Ainsmith succeeded in doing was to turn Dorothy Ferguson into an outfielder. "We were playing in Racine," she says, "and Lois Florreich and Snooky Harrell and Dottie Kamenshek said, 'Come out and eat with us.' So we were all sitting there with the manager, and suddenly one of them said, 'Dottie, how would you like to play in the outfield?' I thought, 'This is all planned—I know it.' So the next night I was in center field. I thought I was being demoted, but once I got out there, you couldn't get me back. When I had been at second, I couldn't ease up. I'd throw too hard, no matter what the distance. Now I had room. Boy, did I have room. I covered right, left and second base. You should have seen me run."

In Peoria, meanwhile, the players were mounting a revolt, led by Faye Dancer. Midway through the season, having touched bottom in the standings, they blamed Johnny Gottselig, who, according to Dancer, "had got to the point where he didn't even care about the team any more." After a game in Kenosha, someone was delegated to call a Redwings board member and demand a meeting. When the team arrived back home, they marched to the stadium and convened a gathering involving most of the players, the board of directors and a startled Gottselig. The players listed their many grievances, while Gottselig sat in silence. After which, says Dancer, "the board fired him then and there," replacing him with Leo Schrall. It wasn't, however, the last time Gottselig was to manage a League team.

The world outside the League's ballparks was changing daily. Most of the servicemen were back, standing in line for a finite number of jobs. The end of gas rationing and travel restrictions meant that fans now could and did go to Chicago or Milwaukee to watch the major-leaguers. The home-field bleachers began to lose their allure.

Some players, aware of these developments, decided it was high time to make their mark as entrepreneurs. Connie Wisniewski and Doris Satterfield opened The Chicks Dugout, a hole-in-the-wall burger joint. After the last picture show, Grand Rapids moviegoers from the theater down the street dropped by for a late-night hotdog or a hamburger and fries. Wisniewski was a quick study, learning her short-order skills from the landlord, who also owned a drugstore and soda fountain: "He showed me how to make these things. I probably had about two evenings training." This venture was an off-season job; obviously you couldn't superintend a hot stove while playing 120-odd games of baseball. But it was successful, and the partners eventually sold it for a profit.

Meanwhile, in Racine, Joanne Winter had a similar idea. "I figured I'd arrived," she says, "and I thought I'd capitalize on my name." Her father advised her to investigate the candy business, and she took his advice, with Mildred Wilson, the chaperon, as her partner. Wisconsin abounds in German candy-makers. Winter and Wilson made the rounds and settled on Barkdall's in Milwaukee, considered by chocolate connoisseurs to be the nation's best. Barkdall had a long-standing rule: he only sold direct from his factory. But, impressed by the businesslike Belles, "he sold us two boxes of vanilla creams, and that was our start. He got to like us, and we plagued him, and he started selling us anything we wanted. We used his creams and chocolate-covered cherries. Then we got Louis's chocolate-covered nuts from Kenosha. We called the shop 'Joanne Winter, A Finer Candy.' It was tiny, just forty-five square feet, right on the main street. We didn't mind telling people where we got our stock. After all, it was excellent, from these champion candy-makers." Winter eventually dared to make some stock herself, including divinity and peanut brittle, while her father made the fudge. "It was a lot of hard work," she says, "but when you're not afraid of that, it's a lot of fun."

This agreeable enterprise lasted until 1951, when Mildred Wilson succumbed to the attentions of a doctor who rented offices in the same building. "I used to tell people I lost the shop in a poker game," says Winter, "but we just folded it up when Mildred got married."

Meanwhile, the League was pursuing its latest rule change. This season saw the introduction of a full, as opposed to modi-fied, sidearm delivery. It wasn't mandatory; you could still throw underhand if you wanted. "But," says Winter, "it behooved you to throw as hard and as fast as you could, with as much stuff on it as possible. They kept pushing the distance back, too, so it got tougher and tougher." Tough or not, Winter threw well, winning almost as many games as Mildred Earp, 1947's leading pitcher.

Connie Wisniewski converted, too, biting her lip against the pain. "But my ball would sail," she says. "It would just take off—the catcher couldn't catch it, I threw it so hard." Her best seasons had been 1945 and 1946; both years she'd won the pitching championship. But in 1947, she found that she "simply couldn't do it. It hurt my arm every time. But if I threw underhand, I couldn't expect to compete with the side-armers." That was the problem—the more variety in your grab-bag of pitches, the most advantage you had. In 1947, Wisniewski won a mere sixteen games, losing almost as many— a bitter blow. "I think the hardest thing for me was the first time I was taken out of a game," she says. "The manager would come out and ask me if I thought I could do it. I'd say, 'If you think you've got somebody better, put 'em in. But if you're asking me if I'm ready to come out, then no, I'm not.' But I know Millie Earp and Alice Haylett saved a couple of games for me. If I'd stayed in, we'd have lost." That knowledge—that she couldn't deliver her best—hurt Wisniewski the most.

So fortunes ebbed and flowed. In the course of a crucial play-off game, Tex Lessing, the Grand Rapids catcher, made headlines by going after an umpire. Lessing was accurately described by Dottie Hunter as "cute as a bug's ear." This did not diminish her fighting spirit.

The Chicks were locked in an eighth-inning 2-2 tie with Racine. The bases were loaded, and a runner was about to be sacrificed home by Choo Choo Hickson. The play was close, but the official called it safe. "In a split second," said a captivated newspaper reporter, "Lessing pounced on umpire George Johnson with both hands flying and slugged him so hard in the eye and face that he staggered back under the attack, so dizzy he was unable to continue working behind the plate." Lessing was (not surprisingly) booted out of what remained of the game, and considered herself lucky to escape without a suspension. The Belles, their morale boosted by the win, went on to capture the championship, and Johnson's fellow officials opted for leniency. Play-off pressure, they said, might get to anyone. Lessing was fined $100—a punishment blunted when Grand Rapids fans raised $2,000 on her behalf, in payment for granting their fondest wish at last.

1948

THE LAST ASCENDING SEASON

Somewhere, way off in the world of big-league baseball, Joe DiMaggio was signed by the New York Yankees for $65,000 and bonuses. The Cleveland Indians paid $87,000 for ace pitcher Bob Feller. The weekly budget for an entire All-American team was $4,000. DiMaggio and Feller went to the bank; the All-Americans went to Opa-Locka, Florida.

Its ball field—a change, at least, from the rigors of Pascagoula, though a slight comedown from 15,000 frenzied Cubans—showed signs of recent manicuring. The players faced Johnny Rawlings, sprung for the occasion from his duties with the Grand Rapids Chicks and ready to lead them through their first exercise of the day. Already their faces felt the warmth of the Florida sun. Most players had smeared white zinc paste on their noses, hoping to protect against blisters. Before the week was out, many would have their first sunburn of the season.

They had left Chicago's Union Station in the middle of a snowstorm. The rookies, having made their connections from small towns near and far, had worried that they'd get lost in its echoing depths, or miss their train. They needn't have worried. Even Christine Jewett, fresh from rural Saskatchewan, had no trouble finding her way. "The station was wall-to-wall girls," she says, "all headed for the same platform. There were two or three carloads full. I just followed the crowd." The train pulled into Miami well past midnight, but the players stayed up for hours in their hotels, renewing old acquaintances or cementing new ones. Now, groggy and train-lagged, they didn't dare show the signs. Even though they had arrived late, they had to report to the field in fighting trim, sharp at ten o'clock.

Opa-Locka, now absorbed into the sprawl of Greater Miami, was an abandoned naval air station, converted after the war to more pleasurable use. The grounds contained several playing fields, but only one was large enough to hold the 160 players, including 40 rookies. The League was once again on the expansion trail—this time, to Springfield, Illinois, and for the first time to Chicago itself. The result was a record ten teams, divided for the first time into two divisions, east and west. They would play the longest League schedule ever—126 games, not including play-offs.

While Rawlings kicked off the exercise session, Max Carey stood on the sidelines conferring with League officials. These men were there to decide which of the rookies and how many veterans would be assigned to the expansion teams—the Springfield Sallies and the Chicago Colleens. They stood side-by-side with the chaperons and a group of local club directors, there to get their first look at the new crop.

A hundred players had come down on the previous night's train. Sixty more would arrive by week's end, but all the pitchers and catchers were in the first wave. They needed all the preparation time they could get, to familiarize themselves with the 1948 season's bold new innovation, the overhand pitch. This year, Carey was bound and determined to erase the last suspicion that girls' baseball was still softball in disguise. For insurance, Carey had also changed everything else—the pitching distance, the basepath length and the size of the regulation ball. Pitchers and catchers had been experimenting with these modifications over the winter months using a smaller ball sent them by the League. Now was the time to try it out for real.

Photographers had set up tripods and heavy cameras at strategic points around the field. One newsman, anxious to gain a unique perspective, was lying flat on the ground in the path of a row of players who ran obligingly towards him. The click of cameras and the scratch of pencils on notebooks would make a steady background accompaniment to training over the next two weeks.

Carey and the officials studied the rookies with an appraising and practiced eye. The League usually rejected four out of five new players. This year, however, it was short of veterans to shuffle around and couldn't afford to be too picky. For the benefit of the press and the home-town fans, Carey was optimistic. "It looks as if our tryout schools are paying off," he announced. "The time we spent culling over scouting reports is going to pay big dividends. Right at the moment, I haven't seen more than one or two girls who will be sent back for more experience, and that is most unusual."

In fact, much of the media attention centered not on unknown quantities, but on the return of veteran players who'd quit or taken time off in previous seasons. The League had made an all-out push to coax retired players back into pro ball. Some had refused to reconsider. The All-American dispatched an emissary to Toronto in an effort to persuade Gladys "Terrie" Davis, 1943's batting champion, to return. Traded by Jack Kloza to appease his Rockford dugout, she had bounced from the Chicks to the Muskegon Lassies, for whom she played first base in 1946. The next season she'd stayed in Ontario where, despite the emissary's urgings, she would remain.

Several married players had decided to spend more time on the home front in 1945; now, they were filtering back. Dorothy Wiltse, the California pitcher (now known by her married name of Dottie Collins) was among them. Bonnie Baker was absent from spring training yet again, but had promised to report to South Bend for opening day. Perhaps the biggest news was that Pat Keagle, "the Blonde Bombshell," who'd left in 1946, was coming back. Keagle had not been idle. She had kept her hand in with the Arizona Queens. She showed up in Opa-Locka "in flashy sunbelt sportswear," but carrying ten extra pounds. "Sure, I'm overweight," she said, "but I can lose that quick." Keagle was widely popular, and her return perked everyone up.

And Allington was back with Rockford. He had settled, for the moment, his feud with Snooky Harrell. The two foes had reached an uneasy detente during the winter months, in the course of dinner at a Los Angeles restaurant. "My mother warned me," says Harrell. "She said, 'He's going to be so nice to you, and you're going to agree to go back.'" And by the end of the evening, sure enough, Allington had won her over. "Then," says Harrell, "we all went out that next Sunday to practice in Pasadena. Pepper and Faye and Tiby were there, and Allington was as snotty as ever." This had infuriated Harrell all over again. She wrote to the League's business manager, asking to be placed on another team—any other team, as long as it was miles away from Allington. But her conscience began to bother her. "I had joined church," she says, "and I felt that I should make an attempt to play for Bill again. I felt a responsibility as a Christian to try to get along with him." During spring training, she was temporarily assigned to the Colleens, but when the final choices were made, she was back on the Rockford roster.

A combination of excitement and apprehension gripped the players. Some feared that they wouldn't make the grade, and they were right. Christine Jewett remembers one young recruit, from Moose Jaw, Saskatchewan, who didn't stay the course. "One night, when we got together for supper, she wasn't there. Somebody said they'd told her she wasn't going to make it, and they'd just gone ahead and made arrangements and she disappeared. I knew of two or three others like that. One by one they were told they didn't make it, and then they'd be gone." By the time it got to the last day or two, most of these cuts had been made.

This year, as always, the players sweated and groaned through the tough workouts. The Californians could frolic on a beach during the off-season, but players who returned each winter to frigid climates lived more sedentary lives. Doris Satterfield, the nursing graduate, was fitter than most, but admits that no one would have survived the season without the spring training ritual: "It was intense exercise. I know that the first year, I couldn't get out of bed in the mornings. My legs were black and blue. We weren't even allowed to ride an elevator. If our room was on the fifth floor, we walked up and down the stairs. Somebody dropped a quarter one night, but decided not to pick it up. She kicked it aside, saying, 'It's just not worth it.'"

By the time Allocation Day rolled around, the League had made its choices. This year, the rules had been toyed with more than usual, mostly to make sure the expansion teams fielded able rosters and that pitchers were well distributed. The best teams were allowed to retain a core of eight players from the year before, but only two could be pitchers. Second-ranked teams were allowed to keep nine, also with two pitchers. But no team would be assigned any additional players from the reserve pool until the Colleens and Sallies had drawn seven players each. One sportswriter summed up the general attitude: "When the league's own rules are not sufficient to equalize the teams, then a new rule is adopted forthwith to do the job." But they didn't know the half of it. Dismay would intensify in June when there was a second, sudden reallocation based on the early-season standings.

Some players had nothing to fear from the allocation process. Dottie Kamenshek, the Rockford Peaches' first baseman, didn't have much to worry about. About to start her fifth season with the League, she was generally acknowledged as its best all-round player. She was from Cincinnati, where her family had struggled through the Depression. The memory of hard times had spurred her to think about what to do when playing days were over. She had shrewdly banked her salary and would eventually enrol in university. But she felt that she had a good many years left with the Peaches. "I didn't think Rockford would put me on the block," she says, "but I could see other people being nervous."

Dottie Hunter viewed the impending forced marches with gloom. "Everybody would be chewing their nails all night long, wondering what team they were going to," she says. "There was a lot of unhappiness in some places." Hunter and the other chaperons would have to deal with it, comforting those players who had been sent against their will to other teams. Their hurt and rejection ran deeper than anyone imagined. When players were traded away from towns and teams where they had come to feel at home, they felt betrayed and abandoned. Twi Shively had been fielding with the Grand Rapids Chicks for three years and was shocked to discover that she was being sent to the Colleens. The League had its reasons: "They told me I was picked because I had played in Chicago [with the Rockolas, a Chicago League franchise], and I would probably be a drawing card there." She didn't agree, and it made for bitter feelings.

Just prior to allocation day, speculation was rife in the sports pages of the All-American's cities. If Carey was intent on weakening the most outstanding teams, the Muskegon Lassies, who'd topped the 1947 standings, and the Racine Belles, who'd won the championships, had the most to fear. Muskegon fans suspected that the rule limiting each team to two pitchers from the previous year had been designed specifically to thwart the Lassies, who had a clutch of first-rate hurlers.

Muskegon's local newspaper, after reviewing the options, was certain that their third baseman would be kept at any cost: "A flock of local fans would howl mur-der if Arleene Johnson, the steady-throwing third sacker, isn't retained." Johnson, from Odema, Saskatchewan (population 500), was a soft-voiced, freckle-faced girl who didn't fit her nickname, "The Iron Lady," given to her for appearing in 224 consecutive games during 1946 and 1947. She was a tremendous favorite with the kids of Muskegon. Nevertheless, despite cries of "Mur-der," Johnson was temporarily lost to the Fort Wayne Daisies (she would soon be shipped back in a reshuffle).

Grand Rapids pundits were equally certain that Connie Wisniewski would remain with the Chicks, even though her pitching days were over. In this case the pundits were right. Of the thirty players shuffled around, eight were from Grand Rapids, but Wisniewski wasn't among them.

Nor did the League's crop of rookies pan out exactly as hoped. By scrambling existing teams, the League had to add only ten new faces. One was Earlene Risinger, known as "Beans" for her beanpole-thin physique. She had read about the League the previous year and tried out in Oklahoma City, where the All-Americans played an exhibition game on the way back from Cuba. Her talent was apparent, and she'd been signed and instructed to report to the League's Chicago office before joining the Rockford Peaches.

But she was only a teenager, and had never traveled any-where in her life. Homesickness hit her hard. As soon as the train pulled into Union Station, she went to the ticket office and bought a seat back to Oklahoma. Far from being a tragedy, it proved a blessing in disguise. "It was a miracle," she says. "They were still pitching underhand and sidearm then, and I was strictly an overhand pitcher. The Lord works in mysterious ways." She went back to picking cotton to repay the money she'd borrowed to go to Chicago. In 1948, the League, undismayed by her last-minute bolt for home the previous year, sent her a recruiting letter. Risinger borrowed more money and set off again. This time she overcame her homesickness and, with her overhand talents at a premium, remained with the Grand Rapids Chicks for seven years.

The ball season that began when the players left Opa-Locka in late April was going to be played in a very different world. Rationing had ended. No more full-page advertisements urged people to work harder, give more blood, buy more bonds. Brand-new cars, snub-nosed and sleek-backed, were once again available. The latest toy was television. And fans had fresh reasons for wanting an escape from reality. Just as war had brought sudden, radical changes, so had peace; by 1948 people were feeling the effects.

Almost all the armed forces had by now been ferried back, and hundreds of thousands of men were in search of work. Industries, with varying degrees of success, were shifting gears away from war production. A baby boom was underway. Inflation was unnerving everyone. Workers were taking to the picket lines in search of raises to cover spiraling costs. The "let's pull together" wartime spirit had disappeared. The League's players made it to their team cities just a few days before a national strike deadline by railway workers, who threatened to bring almost every train in the country to a halt. President Truman had to pass legislation to forestall the strike and keep the trains running.

On the international scene, the Cold War had begun, a Middle East conflict was brewing over the creation of the state of Israel and the U.S. was testing atomic weapons on remote Pacific atolls.

Inspired by postwar change and expectations of even greater crowds, the All-American cities had been indulging in a burst of renovation of their ball fields. The Kenosha Comets moved inland to Simmons Field, well away from the lakefront's unstable weather. The Blue Sox were now at Playland Park, which sat twice as many fans as had the Bendix field. Grand Rapids had launched a $60,000 expansion of their ballpark, a fair portion of which was paid for by the Chicks, who'd been drawing 4,000 people nightly. Now there were an extra two thousand seats, new right-field bleachers, a raised grandstand and an enlarged outfield, which increased the chances of in-the-park triples. Players got improved dugouts and the lighting system was upgraded.

Grand Rapids could well afford these upgrades. Dottie Hunter remembers that nothing seemed impossible during the team's heyday. "In the first years, we were so successful in this town," she says. "We were making money hand over fist."

But the weather was not as sunny as the team's prospects. It was raining and cold; many fields were flooded out. The All-American circuit was not large; if it poured rain in one city, chances were that it poured rain in the rest. These delays would play havoc with the 1948 schedule. Clubs made plans to soak their infields with gasoline and set them ablaze to burn off the moisture, in order to make the opening-day date of Sunday, May 9. Everyone stood peering at the leaden skies.

The midwest must have been a depressing contrast for the players arriving from the sunny south. When one of Rockford's seven daily trains pulled into town, it carried the Peaches, looking "bronzed and in the pink of condition." With only a day or two of enforced rest—given the fact that the playing surface was a bog—they would be ready to launch themselves on yet another season. High prices and the woes of unemployment were forgotten. The girls of summer were back in town, and the good times could start to roll.

And so the season began, in shaky fashion. Once again, expansion—this time to Springfield and Chicago—would almost immediately prove a costly error. In 1944, when Minneapolis and Milwaukee folded, Wrigley had picked up the tab. This time, under the terms of their arrangement with Meyerhoff's Management Corporation, the clubs would be jointly liable for any shortfall. They were rightly concerned that losses in the expansion cities would sabotage their own attempts at solvency. Meyerhoff had told them that the League must expand or die. Critics, including the acerbic Dr. Dailey, argued that adding more clubs would simply increase expenses, with no guarantee that the anticipated extra revenues would be enough to cover them.

Dailey and his fellow detractors were right. By this time, it should have been obvious that an All-American franchise succeeded because of a simple formula: sound management and strong local backing in a small community. Springfield did not qualify. The Sallies were owned by one man, James Fitzpatrick, who also owned the stadium. He had built the ballpark as a war memorial and named it for his son, who'd been killed in action overseas. But Fitzpatrick had funded it through public subscription. The public was less than impressed to learn that they'd have to pay full fare to attend All-American games. In fact, Springfield was a last-minute choice. It had been accepted primarily to make up an even number of teams, which simplified the schedule, and balanced the long-planned entry of Chicago.

Chicago was plainly a unique situation. The League had seen the enormous potential of a franchise there since 1943. It was awash with softball teams; a baseball team should have found a home among hundreds of thousands of fans. But no such luck. The Colleens were run by a Roman Catholic parish, which hoped that the club would set a good example for urban youth. The organizers' hearts were in the right place; the

Colleens almost certainly weren't. They were managed by Dave Bancroft, a former major-leaguer who deserved a more serious treatment from the local press than he got. A typical newspaper feature—in the home of some of the toughest softballers in the country—ran thus: "To be blunt about it, 'Banny' was managing a girl team, and he had to consult the chaperon of his charges to find out if his pitcher felt fit (after a rather long afternoon visit to the beauty parlor) to take the mound against the Muskegon Lassies. Fortunately, the pitcher was ready and willing and looking cute, with long, fluffy hair billowing from under her green cap."

Meyerhoff tried everything he could think of to salvage the team—including arranging television coverage of its games, a League first (although games had been broadcast on the radio in Racine, Muskegon and Grand Rapids). The Chicago broadcasts, sponsored by the Patricia Stevens Modelling School, succeeded only in encouraging people to stay at home and watch.

Wrapped in bright-red jackets, the Rockford Peaches were in the dugout waiting to start their first game of the 1948 season. They had just spent half an hour warming up. Blankets were piled high, ready to ward off the deepening chill. They'd tossed the ball around, splashed mud on their socks and got it wedged between their cleats. Every year, the All-American season had kicked off cold and wet, but 1948 was the worst year on record. It was nearly dark, and the air threatened more rain. If they didn't play tonight's game, it would be the third time their home opener had been postponed. It was the same story all around the League. Most teams had yet to play a game.

The year before, in Allington's absence, the Peaches had fallen apart. Now "The Silver Eagle" was back, raising both hopes and hackles in Rockford: hopes that his winning-is-everything style would bring the city another pennant; hackles among those players who thought his tactics could lose games just as readily as win them.

Allington sat in the dugout beside Dorothy Hunter. Snooky Harrell chose a seat at the far end of the bench. Dottie Ferguson, the wide-ranging outfielder, looked dubiously at the grounds. Her fellow outfielders, Rose Gacioch and Rita "Junior" Briggs, were huddled nearby. Ruth Richard stooped over her catcher's equipment, while Nicky Fox, the starting pitcher, sat nearby.

Stop a person on the street and whisper "baseball" and you'll conjure up images of bright-green diamonds, shimmering in the heat of perfect summer afternoons. Rockford was a far cry from that vision. Regular-season games—except for weekend double-headers—were played in twilight on shadowy fields, as stadium lights took over and weakly imitated the departing sun. That night in Rockford, the temperature was a mere ten degrees above freezing. The Peaches wore dark-colored long-sleeved shirts under their new (and snow-white) home-field uniforms. On nights like these, their skirts seemed more inappropriate than ever.

Across the field, in the third-base dugout, the Chicago Colleens, under Dave Bancroft, were preparing to play their first regular-season All-American League game. They had shown a fair degree of promise during the pre-season exhibition schedule, which wasn't surprising, because the lineup contained only two rookies. All the rest were veterans, wrenched from their former teams by the hated allocation process. Many of them, like Twi Shively, harbored strong resentment. As a result, the team hadn't coalesced, and its morale was low.

At 7:30, the scheduled game time, the contest started. And just as well. The stands, by now in murky darkness and every degree as cold as the dugouts, contained a scant one thousand paying customers, shivering in bleachers that could hold six times that number. Many had come prepared with umbrellas, blankets and bundled-up kids. Fathers and mothers nursed steaming cups of coffee from thermos bottle caps. As a result of the weather, the customary opening-game hoopla was cut short, as though no one was anxious to tempt the rain any further. A local band wheezed through "The Star-Spangled Banner" while both teams stood to attention. The mayor, in natty fedora and his best grey pinstripe suit, threw out the first ball.

The Peaches' defense ran onto the field, each player's name crackling from the loudspeakers. Nicky Fox threw a couple of warm-up pitches to Ruth Richard and the game began. It would be the fans' first chance to witness the overhand throw. The battle was at the mound, and Fox was prepared. She was one of the All-American's original draftees (as Helen Nicol) and had twice been named League pitching champ, in 1943 and 1944, both years with the Kenosha Comets. Her specialty was the wrist ball, a throw that got its increased velocity by means of a twisting action just before release. This style was rare enough that people thought it unique to Canadians. Fox had found it difficult to convert to a sidearm delivery, but had the overhand pitch under control. She lasted seven innings, throwing mostly puzzling curves, and held the Colleens to three runs. She was relieved by the twenty-one-year-old Lois Florreich.

Many batters dreaded facing Florreich, who coupled incredible speed with an alarming lack of control. Tonight, however, the cold had slowed her down. In fact, it was Betty Tucker, the Chicago pitcher, who managed to hit three Peaches (Ferguson, Kamenshek and Rose Gacioch) and walk seven. "Taking one for the team" was Ferguson's specialty. She was a weak batter but could usually get on base by moving herself into the path of the ball. One season, she did so a record-setting ninety-two times. She'd also worked out an interesting sign with Kamenshek, who followed her in the batting order. If she flipped her pigtails, she was about to steal.

Meanwhile, errors played their part, particularly in the rain-soaked infield. Even the usually efficient team of Harrell and Kamenshek logged their share of bobbles. The Colleens showed real strength, compensating for Tucker's weak pitching with a pair of excellent double plays. But, in the end, hitting power held sway. Harrell and Wilma Briggs smacked three doubles between them, and Ruth Richard hit a triple to the right-field fence. When the smoke cleared, Rockford had whipped the Colleens 12-3. Bill Allington was mightily pleased. The result was a good omen for his return. The Chicago team took their defeat in stride. None of the Colleens realized that this was about as good as it was going to get.

Five All-American League cities had scheduled opening games for Sunday, May 9. Ironically, the only city dry enough to hold a game as planned was Springfield, where a Sallies-Fort Wayne Daisies matchup drew four thousand people, despite mixed feelings toward team owner James Fitzpatrick.

As driving rain continued to play havoc with the schedule, other clubs got the impression that the season would never begin. Everyone was anxious to discern a pattern. Who would set the pace? Would it be (as many people believed) Grand Rapids? Under the sober Johnny Rawlings, the Chicks had done well in 1947. This was his third year in command; he was a force to be reckoned with. Or would the Racine Belles reprise their championships of 1946 and 1947? With Allington back in Rockford, a number of observers were betting on the Peaches, while others maintained that this would finally be South Bend's year. Harold Dailey liked to point out that the Blue Sox franchise had done all the right things—giving up veterans to allocation, backing its manager against fractious players, launching massive ticket-selling drives resulting in League-leading attendance. Despite all this, he said—and because of the League's refusal to give South Bend quality players in return—the Blue Sox, the League's perennial brides-maids, had been cheated of the championship season after season. Maybe this year their time had come at last.

It was hard to build anticipation during the season's early weeks. News reports centered endlessly on the abysmal weather. Depending on the writer's point of view, the ceaseless rain either excused low attendance or pointed up the raw courage of those fans who braved freezing temperatures. In Muskegon—not a prime contender for the championship—the local newspaper attempted to rally the faithful. The Lassies' fans were noted for their loyalty, but this year, faced with a depleted team, their patience was sorely tried. An editorial harked back to the glory days at Marsh Field, pointing up baseball's value as an entertainment where anything goes. "Last year at one of the games," it read, "the fans had an opportunity to watch a Lassie rally at the plate in the ninth inning, a building burning across the street and a trouble-maker being dragged bodily from the stands by two burly guards—all this at the same time and at no extra charge." It wasn't what you would call Triple-A publicity, but at least it got the Lassies' name spelled right.

As May gave way to June and the weather at last improved, a pattern began to emerge. As expected, the established clubs had come to dominate the standings. Grand Rapids set the pace in the eastern division, while Rockford headed the west, by a conspicuous margin. The Springfield Sallies were performing dismally—no hope for them—but, then again, nobody had expected very much. All eyes were on the Chicago Colleens. Despite good players and the services of the experienced Bancroft, they were at the bottom of the western division. They weren't simply bad, they were terrible, having played fourteen games and registered only a single win.

Carey and Meyerhoff went into a panic. If Chicago failed, it would prove beyond all doubt that the League couldn't cut it in major-league cities, and that the dissenters had been right all along. The League's response was to take the Colleens apart and put them together again. Carey presented a new resolution to the allocation board, suggesting specific "emergency trades"—to be made without the managers' approval, although he had talked matters over with the club directors. He maintained that such trades "will not hurt the ability of any club to win, and will put a ball club on the field in Chicago which can compete with the rest of the League." The board must have approved his plan, which went into effect on June 1, as requested. Chicago got what amounted to an entirely new team, composed of players dragooned from all the other clubs. Only Springfield was left untouched.

The Grand Rapids Chicks lost ace shortstop Ernestine "Teeny" Petras, part of their prized double-play combination. Dottie Hunter remembers that "it had to be either Teeny or Zig [Alma Ziegler]. Well, Zig was captain and had been forever. So Teeny had to go." The only happy note was struck when the Fort Wayne Daisies decided to send Arleene Johnson back to the Muskegon Lassies. A great many players were sent scurrying to and fro in this massive—though in the end fruitless—exercise. But, with the exception of Rita Briggs, an outfielder with the Rockford Peaches, none of the players who were parachuted into Chicago did particularly well. They could not salvage the Colleens' miserable fortunes.

In fact, all that the board's machinations accomplished was to confirm many people's worst fears. Ever since the days of Philip Wrigley's benevolent dictatorship, the League's critics had sought more power in the hands of individual clubs. Wrigley had at least commanded respect. Meyerhoff and Carey, on the other hand, could not make the clubs pull together. Unless Chicago showed immediate improvement and began to pull its weight, the men responsible for its place in the League would have another strike against them.

And what of the introduction of the overhand throw? Why did the League insist on it anyway? Because deep in the hearts of the All-American's organizers was a primary allegiance to "real" baseball. Max Carey, despite his reaction to the 1946 play-offs, saw the All-American's lack of tradition as something to be taken advantage of. "It is our obligation to go forward instead of standing still or going backward," he said. "It has taken men's baseball fifty years to settle on its distances and rules. We have made tremendous strides in five years, and feel that we are well on our way to accomplishing our aims—to bring about the best looking sports spectacle in as short a time as possible."

And so the pitchers struggled afresh. Joanne Winter had learned to cope with the sidearm delivery just in time for it to become obsolete. A sidearm pitch—full, modified or disguised with something plucked from a bag of tricks—was outmoded overnight. A good overhand throw would beat it every time. Winter wasn't totally unprepared; she'd made one succesful transition already. Nor were many other pitchers. Most of them had tried the overhand in sandlot games as they were growing up. And a fielded ball was always thrown that way. "But," says Winter, "although I had a good arm, I'd never used it as a stressful pitching motion for that number of innings and throws in a row. It's a much more difficult physical maneuver, but I thought it was a challenge. I was kind of excited to see if I could do it."

In fact, there wasn't any option. During the winter months, the League had sent all the pitchers a supply of new, slightly smaller balls (which now measured ten and three-eighths inches). As for the overhand throw, the instruction was: "You'd better get used to it." Winter wasn't concerned—at least at first: "When you're twentysomething, you don't worry as much."

After a winter's practice at the local YWCA, Winter had barely kicked off the season, under the watchful eye of Racine's manager, Leo Murphy, when she discovered that she had a relatively rare medical condition. She was born with an extra lumbar vertebra, which had fused to the next one in line. Her former pitching habits hadn't aggravated it. Now, throwing overhand for any length of time caused the extra vertebra to slip and cause severe pain. Doctors suggested an operation, which Winter refused. "They wanted to open up my back, take some bone off my fibula and graft it and—oh, my God!—the procedure they described was three pages of typewritten stuff and it scared me to death." Instead, she opted for the advice offered by another doctor, whom Mildred Wilson, the club chaperon and Winter's business partner, had recommended. His solution was somewhat more straightforward: simply tape the offending vertebra in place.

So it was that, before every game, Wilson would criss-cross Winter's entire back with a roll of surgical tape, cinching her in like a mummy: "Towards the end of the game, when I got a little heated, it would work loose and I would feel that dog-gone pain in the coccyx, but I would muster through it. You just ride through it, and we didn't have a lot of painkillers in those days."

As a result of these primitive expedients, Winter continued to throw—and throw extremely well. Nor did she publicize the true extent of her condition. It became general knowledge during spring training that she had a "crick" in her back; that was all. In early June, she and the Belles traveled to South Bend. In front of 4,500 Blue Sox fans, Winter pitched superbly, winning 5-1. A local sports editor, unaware of the fact that she'd thrown, as always, in some pain, suspected tales of her bad back had been a ruse to deceive the opposing team. "Winter threw sharp-breaking hooks and smoky fast balls past the Blue Sox with such deadly effect that she retired twenty-four hitters without one of them reaching first," he wrote. "She fanned twelve, didn't give a walk after she passed Shoo-Shoo Wirth to open the game, and received the benefit of perfect support throughout. Maybe a good backache would help out some of the Blue Sox pitchers."

Generally speaking, most players coped remarkably well with 1948's rampant rule changes. But there were some misgivings. Some mourned the loss—now absolute—of windmill pitchers, who had delivered balls with sweeping, ferris-wheel swoops. Joanne Winter cites another hazard: the new, smaller ball came off a bat that much quicker. On the mound, having completed your delivery, you were vulnerable: "I felt that we weren't going to be up to it, to have someone jamming that ball back at us as hard as they could hit it." And other perils lurked. A skilled pitcher, having mastered the overhand throw, could make a smaller, harder, faster-moving ball do more. Thrown by erratic hurlers, it became a threat. These were the days before the batting helmet, and hitters were justifiably leery of beanballs thrown by accident or with intent.

Otherwise, the game was zippier, more complex. It called for subtle, almost unconscious adaptations. Arleene Johnson found that "the strategy changed slightly, because the delivery was different. Base-running depended on the pitcher's wind-up and presentation—all of which altered with an overhand pitch." The game changed, but opinions differ as to whether it changed for the better.

It meant a wholesale shift in the fortunes of a team's pitching staff. The League knew that certain players would be unable to adapt. Perhaps they could be relocated, and some, like Connie Wisniewski, were. She went to the outfield and concentrated on hitting, but continued to pitch from time to time; she was allowed ten starts a season. Her first was in June, in the course of an inconsequential series against the Springfield Sallies. In the second game of a double-header, she had a rocky first inning, during which the Sallies scored twice. Wisniewski settled down, but lost 3-2. It didn't endanger the Chicks' first-place standing, but it was a humiliating defeat. Fortunately, Wisniewski's value to the Chicks could be read in her batting statistics. In 1948, she ranked third in all the League. Other pitchers went into the discard file.

Oddly enough, the League actually thought that the overhand toss might alleviate the chronic pitcher shortage. There was a considerable reservoir of unused talent in the infield and the outfield. Perhaps some of these players—who tossed overhand as a matter of course—could be retrained. And this was correct, to some degree. Betsy Jochum was a five-year veteran in 1948, a mainstay of the South Bend Blue Sox. She was a solid hitter, and had done particularly well in 1944, winning the batting championship. When the underhand throw arrived, she—like anyone else with a vaguely reasonable arm—was given a chance on the mound, and she rejuvenated her career in this new position.

Her first chance as a starter came on a chilly Saturday night near the end of May, when South Bend hosted the Fort Wayne Daisies. The final score was 6-0—not bad for a maiden outing. And just as well. Jochum's emergence as a pitcher with unusual speed and remarkable control came at a time when South Bend's pitching staff was riddled with injuries. Elsewhere, others made the transition work. Lois Florreich was another outfielder, one of the League's original players. She'd started with South Bend in 1943, and moved from third base to center field at the urging of manager Bert Niehoff. Traded to Kenosha in mid-1945, she'd continued to prosper in the outfield, began to assume occasional pitching duties in 1946 as a sidearm pitcher, and by 1948—now with the Rockford Peaches—was the fourth-highest-ranked pitcher in the entire League.

One thing was certain: the overhand throw made for less frequent appearances. When Helen Nicol was the top-ranked pitcher in 1943, she played in 47 out of 108 scheduled games. By comparison, Alice Haylett, 1948's pitching leader, was at the mound (sometimes for a couple of innings only) in no more than a quarter of the contests. "Underhand, it never used to hurt," says Connie Wisniewski. "It was effortless. I used my whole body and I could pitch two, three games in a row." No more. Pitchers couldn't last a double-header as they'd done in the old days. In fact, they couldn't last the game. For the first time, relievers were needed in volume; but where were the closers to come from? As the season wore on, the winning pitchers and high-scoring hitters were the same old faces, those who'd been playing the game for many years.

A few short weeks into the 1948 schedule, the All-American's pennant seemed all but won, despite the large-scale shuffle in early June which did nothing except exacerbate ill-will between individual teams and the League's head office. As luck would have it, the first club that the rejuvenated Colleens had to contend with were the League-leading Grand Rapids Chicks, whose lineup included Pepper Paire.

Paire was still up to her old tricks. One week, without permission, she'd driven up to a town called Baldwin to celebrate with fans. She and the fans spent all one afternoon fishing, in what was perfect weather. "I didn't think I'd get burned, because I was used to the California sun," she says. "But in the midwest, playing mostly night games, you don't get much sun." Paire turned up at the clubhouse, red as a lobster. Dottie Hunter looked at her. "If you want to save your neck," said Hunter, "you'd better get your stuff on and get out on that ball field right now." The guilty Paire had even got sunburned on the back of her knees: "I had to strap on shinguards. I had to get down in that squat and try to get back up I don't know how many times all through the game. I couldn't say a word. I couldn't let Johnny Rawlings know what was happening." Dottie Hunter kept Paire's painful secret. "I didn't tell Johnny anything," she says. "He would have raised Cain. But he'd have told Pepper the same thing I did. He'd have made her go in and play."

In any case, the Grand Rapids fans and management—unaware of Paire's ordeal—were in bad humor. The June reallocation had cost them the popular Ernestine "Teeny" Petras. Petras was one of only three original Chicks left (along with Wisniewski and Ziegler). Nate Harkness, the club president, had been moved to write a public plea to fans to accept her departure. "It was a most difficult choice for our directors, Johnny Rawlings and me personally to make," he said. "We had a shortstop with ability, experience and spirit, badly needed at Chicago. Our sense of obligation gave us no choice." An enormous crowd attended the last game Petras played in Chicks' uniform, to say goodbye.

Petras then went to Chicago, where the prospect of an improved team drew larger crowds than usual. The Chicks arrived for a four-game series and won three. Before the reshuffling, the Colleens would have lost the lot. Indeed, the Colleens had picked up a head of steam. They also managed to draw nearly two thousand fans per game. But it was too little, too late. They continued to trail their division by an enormous margin.

Meanwhile, in Springfield, the Sallies stood revealed as a lost cause. By this time, Fitzpatrick had returned the franchise to the League, and the Sallies (as had the Minneapolis Millerettes in 1944) now traveled constantly, a band of orphans, while Max Carey strove to find them a permanent home in some other, more hospitable city. This was intolerable. Carey and Meyerhoff had planned on hot pennant races in both east and west divisions, capped by a three-week round of play-offs that would enable the All-American to reach its long-predicted one-million attendance mark. Instead, the pennant race was confined to the same three or four teams. Chicago was on life-support and Springfield was roaming the back roads; neither club would affect the eventual outcome.

Players dropped out for various reasons. By mid-June, one player had been released for the murky catch-all "disciplinary action." A couple more—both married women—bailed out of their own accord. And, as usual, there were a handful of players who simply didn't measure up.

What would really affect the championship, however, was injuries—the wild card that sent experienced players to the bench, rookies to fill their places and teams to the League's doorstep, crying aloud for replacements. In the course of 1948, Marge Stefani, Rockford's second baseman, was out with a sore leg. Muskegon's outfield lost two first-stringers in a row. South Bend's pitching staff was hurting badly. Bonnie Baker, its star catcher, had arm troubles of her own. Her replacement, Norma Metrolis, had a bad knee. Fort Wayne lost the capable pitcher Annabelle Lee. Then Dottie Collins, its best hope on the mound, announced that she intended to resign at season's end. All this came at the worst possible time, as managers scrambled desperately to find overhand pitchers who could carry a four- or five-game series. No one could foresee how even the old reliables would perform in clutch situations.

As if that weren't enough, the All-American was blindsided at this critical juncture by none other than its old nemesis, the Chicago League. The two bodies had reached an uneasy truce in 1946. This detente was shattered by the All-American's expansion into Chicago itself. The Colleens weren't the violation. It was two minor farm teams set up by the League that the Chicago organization objected to.

The two leagues had met in the spring of 1948 in attempts to resolve their difficulties. Carey wanted to formalize the working agreement because clashes were inevitable; the leagues had butted heads over the same player on a number of occasions. Doris Satterfield had been spotted by the All-American in 1945. While she was still a nursing student, the League had offered her a contract. She'd signed. But, before graduation rolled around, a representative of the Chicago League offered yet another contract. "It was a better contract, so I signed it, too," she says. "Oh, sure, I realized what I was doing. I figured sooner or later it'd work its way out, and it did."

Having made this double-booking, Satterfield reported to the Chicago League and played with one of its teams at a salary of $185 a week. The All-American maximum was still $100. This exposure, she says, gave the All-American a chance to see what she could do without having to pay for the privilege. And Satterfield was hot: "I couldn't do anything wrong. I was just literally on fire. I was leading the [Chicago] League in hitting, in fielding, and all of a sudden the All-American is interested again." When Satterfield refused to honor her original League contract, the All-American applied heavy pressure on the Chicago owners and succeeded in getting Satterfield barred from play. She was reduced to taking a factory job—not for $185 a week. She therefore phoned Carey: "And he couldn't have been nicer. He picked me up, brought me to Grand Rapids, introduced me to the team and I loved it there."

Carey won that round. But he didn't always gain the upper hand. When Bonnie Baker was approached by the Chicago League, she didn't try to hide the fact. When she met with one of the Chicago League officials, she made a point of phoning Carey, to let him know. Carey countered with a lunch date, and dragged along the then-eminent major-league player Rogers Hornsby. Baker was underwhelmed. Carey told her how disappointed he was that she'd even consider leaving the All-American. "Well, Max," she said, "what would you do? Would you leave your team if another one offered you twice as much?" Carey allowed as he might "consider it." "You wouldn't consider it," said Baker. "You'd make a deal." And so—by the time lunch ended—had Carey and Baker. She was free to negotiate a higher salary with the South Bend club—a contravention of the rules, since she was already making more than the maximum, but the price you paid to keep a star catcher and prototypical All-American Girl in the fold.

So it was that, in early 1948, Meyerhoff, Carey and several All-American team presidents (including Nate Harkness of Grand Rapids, Judge Edward Ruetz of Kenosha, Bill Wadewitz of Racine and Dr. Harold Dailey of South Bend) sat down with Archie Wolf, president of the Chicago League. They discussed a formal contract that would regulate recruitment and trade. The All-American pledged not to introduce more than two expansion clubs into Chicago during the next five years. Nor would a second club be established without prior notification to Wolf and the Chicago League owners.

This meeting ended on an uncertain note. Dr. Dailey later wrote that Harkness, who acted as chairman, was the worse for drink, which Dailey suggested had shocked the Chicago League's representatives. This was silly. These men were tough customers; even stumbling drunkenness would not have shocked them. In any case, matters remained unresolved until May, when the All-American chose to alleviate its chronic player shortage by setting up two farm teams, bang in the middle of Chicago. Fred Leo remembers that these enterprises were glorified tryout sessions, held irregularly at best. But the Chicago League, eager perhaps for an excuse to declare open season, revoked the gentleman's agreement, thus raising the specter of widespread raiding one more time.

Here the All-American was vulnerable. It had been trying to reduce costs, and had already imposed salary limits. The Chicago League owners had the edge, because they had more to offer. There wasn't a wholesale desertion from the All-American, but a few more players opted for greener pastures. Added to the League's other woes, it was a simply another problem in a season that had seen more than its share.

By June 1948, the All-American's east and west divisions were headed by the Grand Rapids Chicks and the Rockford Peaches.

The Chicks in particular looked well-nigh unbeatable. Their closest competition was the Fort Wayne Daisies, who were struggling to play .500 ball. In the west, the Peaches had a smaller lead over the team on its tail, the Kenosha Comets. As June ticked away, circumstances changed. The Daisies began to creep up on Grand Rapids, winning almost entirely on the strength of their pitching, led by Dottie Collins. The Daisies' good fortune was augmented by a Grand Rapids slump. When the Chicks and Daisies met for a three-game series, Grand Rapids took the first game, aided by Pat Keagle's speed on the basepaths, but Fort Wayne won the remaining two. The Chicks might have split these contests, but Rawlings handed the pitching chores to rookies who needed the exposure; they also needed more practice; one game was lost 10-1.

This brought the Daisies to within two games of the division leaders going into a series with the much weaker Colleens. But luck took a hand. Soon after, injuries struck half the team, including the invaluable Collins. By mid-July, Grand Rapids was six games ahead of Fort Wayne and the Chicks' lead grew. Any hope the Daisies had of launching another challenge to the Chicks was smashed in late July when Collins announced her immediate retirement. In fact, the Daisies were in danger of losing their play-off berth to the cellar-dwelling Colleens.

In the western division, it was a livelier story. Rockford topped the standings in mid-June, led by the fielding skills of Snooky Harrell and by Dottie Kamenshek's power at the plate. But the Peaches were overtaken by the Peoria Redwings. Within a couple of weeks, both clubs had been displaced by the Racine Belles, whose savvy manager, Leo Murphy, had husbanded his resources and fielded a team of healthy veterans. Murphy and the Racine directors had taken the long view, building a solid roster and resisting the temptation of seemingly advantageous quick-fix trades. As the League entered the final weeks of the season, everyone expected Grand Rapids to top the standings, but no one was sure who it would end up battling for the championship.

Nor were things quiet on the financial front. By 1948, those players who had enlisted in their early twenties, beset now by the aches and pains that signal advancing age, had begun to take stock of their future. They loved to play, but they saw that events were catching up to them. They knew their careers weren't forever. Many had begun to cast a wary eye on their bank balance.

Individual players were reluctant to discuss salaries with their teammates. They knew that certain star players—those with proven fan appeal and drawing power—were getting sometimes huge under-the-table supplements to the supposed weekly maximum of $100. The amounts involved depended on their bargaining position, on how assertive they could be and on the resources of their individual clubs. Negotiations were very private. To this day, players refuse to confirm or deny exactly what they got. Bonnie Baker was supposed to have received at least one $2,500 signing bonus. She denies it was that much, but refuses to name the figure. Dottie Kamenshek, probably the League's most valuable player, confirms that she got $500. Harrell got $100, not as much as she'd been promised.

Such piecemeal special treatment led to wounded feelings, especially since salary increases were subjective in the extreme, based not on performance measured by statistics but on intangible star quality. Betsy Jochum, who'd proven herself a talented outfielder and hitter, was being groomed in 1948 as a pitcher for the South Bend Blue Sox because of her strong arm. Manager Marty McManus told her she deserved more money, and should ask for it. Jochum went to Dr. Dailey, who said that he wasn't allowed to pay her more than the $100 maximum—a blatant lie. Why didn't Jochum get her well-merited raise? "Because I wasn't the personality kid," she says. And it was true. Jochum, an accomplished athlete and well-liked by her peers, lacked the showboat pizzazz of Pat Keagle, Faye Dancer or—above all—Bonnie Baker. "When we'd sign autographs or talk to the fans, Bonnie's name would always come up," says Lou Arnold. This holds true fifty years later. Today, when people recall the Blue Sox, one name is repeated over and over, like a mantra. The refrain is always the same: "Remember Bonnie Baker ..."

Nor was dissatisfaction confined to the balance sheet. Players had begun to look upon their managers with a more jaundiced eye. Some of the managers were more or less immune. Allington and Rawlings, despite their foibles, were men of undeniable achievement. They merited respect. Others, however, did not. As well, players could see that the League was failing to keep its promises on every front. The new recruits weren't up to snuff. More and more stories began to circulate—some true, some wishful thinking—of players lobbying club directors, the manager or local fans. When Leo Murphy, manager of the Racine Belles (who was highly regarded by most of his players), talked about trading Joanne Winter, Sophie Kurys—the team's most valuable player—told him that if Winter went, she would too. Murphy relented, but the moral was not lost. This was not the sort of power players ought to have.

But in spite of the rumors, these revolts, whether individual or organized, were rare. Even though Dr. Dailey left notes to the effect that Tiby Eisen and Mary Rountree had engineered Johnny Gottselig's ouster from Peoria in 1947, the truth is that they'd both been traded well before Gottselig got the boot.

Given these mutterings in the ranks, it's not surprising that the League once again asserted its authority on familiar ground, raising the issue of the players' image. Players who stood up for their rights were plainly not the All-American Girl. In 1948, Chet Grant, then managing the Kenosha Comets,

composed a players' manual intended to reassert the princi-
ples that had inspired and nurtured the League, and to provide a blueprint for its continued success. In it, Grant lists
several problems he saw as posing a threat—particularly "dis-
loyal" behavior, which he further categorized as "tale-bearing,
nagging, cliquing" and nursing grudges. These, he said, should
be punished, and players' conduct should be beyond reproach
year-round, not only during the season.

As the final stretch began, baseball fans witnessed the passing
of a legend. George Herman Ruth, a.k.a. Babe, died on August
16. That evening, the All-American's teams stood to attention,
their heads bared and bowed, as the mournful strains of "Taps"
issued metallically from the loudspeakers.

The season's pace was quickening. In theory (and according to one of the founding premises invoked by Chet Grant), it
mattered not who won or lost, as long as the League provided
wholesome entertainment for the community and its young
people. In reality, winning meant money, and the All-American
was counting every penny.

Unfortunately, although overall attendance had grown,
profits had not. Moreover, both Chicago and Springfield had
been a terrific drain. Some teams had drawn well. Others had
not; their balance sheets were gloomier than ever. As usual,
new and even rosier projections were pinned on the play-offs—
which would be longer than ever before—as a means to boost
attendance figures and inject last-minute cash. At least, since
players received a share of these revenues, it might quiet the
malcontents.

As the days shortened and kids began to twitch at the
prospect of a return to the classroom, every game began to
matter. Tempers flared. In August, Snooky Harrell exchanged
words with Gadget Ward, the long-suffering chief umpire. For
this, she was fined $25. Harrell considered it a bit much for

what she said was a "two-bit argument," but Carey was on the case. He had recently mediated a dispute between Chet Grant and yet another official. The two had repaired to the locker room so they could express themselves more frankly. The argument had turned personal, and Grant, usually a mild-mannered personality, had punched the umpire. Word of this got around, and Carey figured it was time to take Grant at his rulebook word, cracking down both on and off the field.

The season's countless rain delays came back to haunt the schedule, as planners scrambled to make up for canceled games. At one point, South Bend played four double-headers (against two formidable opponents, the Chicks and the Peaches) in as many days, straining its already weakened pitching staff. Harried officials put up a barrage of gate prizes and organized special nights of all descriptions—anything to entice the fans through the turnstiles.

By mid-August, the Racine Belles were leading the western division, and Peoria, inspired perhaps by overflow crowds, were right behind them. Allington's Peaches, for their part, were in third place. It had not been Rockford's most auspicious season. Harrell and Kamenshek had both hit well during the early stages but had fallen in the later season. Very few players managed to consistently bat .300, but Kamenshek almost always did. When she faltered, it spread unease and consternation. Allington benched her for a rest and fiddled with the lineup in search of different combinations that might restore his team's power at the plate. He and Harrell continued to be at odds. When Allington made her captain, he said that she shouldn't mind if he was a little hard on her, to avoid charges of favoritism. Harrell was unconvinced.

Allington was not without a sense of humor. In August, during a game with the Blue Sox, South Bend's second baseman worked the old hidden ball trick, luring Kamenshek into making a run for third, where she was promptly thrown out—

directly under Allington's nose in the coaching box. The press reported that after the game, Allington issued a bulletin announcing "he had fined himself $25 for going to sleep on that moth-eaten trick and allowing one of his players to be caught. He also gave himself a beautiful bawling out at the end of the inning, and wasn't speaking to himself for hours after the game."

And then Rockford began a comeback. In the course of a week-long road trip, they moved up a notch by beating Kenosha and splitting a two-game stand at Peoria, then blew the chance to move into first place by losing to the Redwings on the same day as Racine lost to the Muskegon Lassies. The Lassies, embarking on one of their periodic but ultimately fruitless winning streaks, went on to beat Racine twice more, only to watch Rockford sweep by them and into first place in the western standings.

Then the Fort Wayne Daisies took a hand. Despite their shaky record, they put an end to the Lassies' winning ways, and Racine, faced with easier pickings, moved into first again, with Rockford half a game back. The two teams were scheduled to wrap up the season with a three-game series. Just before the Peaches left Rockford to begin the series in Racine, loyal fans rewarded Allington with a pre-game testimonial, in the course of which he received some luggage and a watch, while a twenty-eight-piece band played a medley of his favorite tunes. Better yet, the Peaches won their game against visiting Muskegon 6-0.

In Racine, the Belles, inspired by home-field advantage, won the first game. To finish in first place, Rockford would have to win both halves of the next night's double-header. Over five thousand fans saw the attempt. Both teams scored one run early in the first game, but Racine broke the tie in the fourth and went on to a decisive 6-1 victory. Allington got to keep his watch.

In Fort Wayne, the Daisies had finished a miserable eighth, and manager Dick Bass's head was on the block. A somewhat romantic aura had surrounded Bass when he became Fort Wayne's manager in 1948, his first year with the League. It was helped by the fact that he was good-looking and, at thirty-nine, still relatively young. His minor-league baseball career had been interrupted in 1942 when he nearly lost his life in a defense plant explosion. Later, a playing injury that led to blood poisoning had ended his playing career.

As a manager, Bass was likeable, but he didn't win games. The Daisies had just missed the championship in 1945 and had been hungering for the League crown ever since. By the end of 1948, the Daisies' hopes for a championship seemed to have evaporated again. Bass's shortcomings as a manager were aggravated, in the eyes of club officials, by his close relationship with one of the players, to whom he was rumored to be engaged. The player in question was Marge Callaghan, from Vancouver. Her younger sister Helen, known because of her hitting power as "The Female Ted Williams," also played in the All-American for a time, but dropped out, married and later gave birth to Casey Candaele of the Houston Astros—possibly the only major-leaguer to follow in his mother's footsteps.

In any case, Marge Callaghan denies that she and Bass were a serious item. She says they never dated and that his fault lay in an excessive interest in women, plural. Be that as it may, Bass was unceremoniously sacked by the club directors. The news was conveyed reluctantly by Harold Greiner, one of the directors. Greiner believed that Bass was doing his best and that he hadn't been unduly influenced by Callaghan. "I want you to know this is the toughest job I've ever had in my life," he told him. "It's just what the board has decided, and I'm the carrier of the news, and damn it, I wish I was someplace else." So did Bass, who was virtually shoved off the bus that would carry the

Daisies to their first play-off encounter. He was replaced as manager by not one but three players—Eisen, Rountree and Vivian Kellogg. It marked the first, but not the last time that the All-American would hand a team's reins to the people who were probably best suited to assume them—the players themselves. Fort Wayne figured that, in eighth place, it had nothing to lose by letting players be manager-for-the-moment. Their tenure lasted only throughout the play-offs. The following season, matters returned to normal.

Now fans and home-town officials could spend a few days alternately looking forward to a lengthy series of play-off games and cursing the system set up by the League. The regular season of 120 games had determined that Racine and Grand Rapids were the top clubs. If they had met immediately in a best-of-five-game contest, it would have made some sense. Instead, with an eye to revenues, the League embarked on what was in essence a mini-season, with only the two worst teams—the Colleens and the Sallies—out of contention. The advantage to the League could be seen in the attendance figures. Even given sell-outs of every game, play-offs between the division leaders would have drawn a maximum of 20,000 fans. By staging twenty-five games, the All-American's coffers were swelled by 75,000 paid admissions. Of course, this start-from-scratch scenario gave the lightweights—Fort Wayne, Kenosha and the perennial bridesmaid, South Bend—another chance to make good.

When the play-offs got underway, Racine rapidly defeated Peoria in the western division, while Rockford polished off Kenosha. In the east, it took Grand Rapids five games to eliminate the Blue Sox, while the Fort Wayne Daisies, who had halted a thirteen-game winning streak by the Muskegon Lassies earlier in the season, faced them again and won.

Racine, minus Sophie Kurys, out of the lineup with an ankle injury, then met Rockford. Kurys' absence tipped the scales, and Rockford won three straight. Fort Wayne, meanwhile, was proving to be the Cinderella story of the series. Having ended the regular season in eighth place, plagued by injuries and with a three-player triumvirate filling in for the sacked Dick Bass, they still managed to defeat the boisterous Grand Rapids Chicks in three straight games. The Chicks' surprising weakness might be attributable in part to the shock of losing Pat Keagle, who had slid into second base and ripped her anklebone from its socket. So severe was her injury that the bone protruded through the skin. She attended the final games on crutches, only to see her teammates lose.

The final series between Rockford and Fort Wayne was a best-of-seven, kicking off at Rockford's Beyer Stadium, then moving to Fort Wayne three games later. Rockford had expanded its capacity to nine thousand seats, and they almost managed to fill them. As it turned out, the Peaches had an easy time of it. Having surprised everyone thus far—including themselves—the Daisies couldn't pull another rabbit out of the hat. They lost the first three contests, won the fourth (Rockford's only loss in the entire play-offs), but lost again, to hand Allington's Peaches the 1948 championship in the fifth and final game.

The next week, Chet Grant, the manual writer, decided to extricate himself from a two-year contract with Kenosha. He went to the team president's office and told Judge Ruetz that he wanted out. "Well, Chet," said Ruetz's assistant, "you did good enough for us to let you resign." Unknown to Grant, the club had already chosen his successor.

1949–1954

✘

THE FINAL INNINGS

No one realized at the end of 1948 that the All-American League had reached its high point. Girls' baseball seemed to be on a roll, riding an ever-upward curve of popularity. Attendance had risen steadily since 1943; surely it would continue to do so. The League made decisions based on this optimistic outlook, but Fred Leo acknowledges that they were whistling in the dark, churning out public relations hype that a close look at hard figures failed to warrant.

But the figures were hard to read; the decline wasn't absolute. Some cities continued to rack up phenomenal attendance, given the size of the population base. The League's head office and the club directors kept telling each other that all their woes were simply growing pains, that a tighter control on the finances would put them in the black. Like prairie farmers, they believed in next year. But they were wrong. The summer of 1948 was the last time the League moved forward. Soon it would slip, slowly at first, and then with ever-gathering momentum.

None of the problems that had plagued the League in 1948 were to be resolved. Training and recruitment procedures failed to provide an adequate number of promising players.

(In 1948, the League had attempted to inject a touch of exotica by recruiting a number of Cuban players who spoke no English and had very little in common with their teammates. Although a couple had successful pro ball careers, most of them finally succumbed to homesickness and left.) Teams were aging in place, relying on long-time veterans. Allocation was almost universally disparaged. Even winning teams believed they'd done well despite, not because of, the system.

Expansion had once again proved a failure. Springfield wound up costing the League thousands of dollars, a bill shared among the other clubs, who could ill afford it. Chicago was also a financial drain, and brought few of the benefits that Meyerhoff had envisioned. He had thought that the smaller cities would get fired up, viewing the Colleens as new, exciting rivals: "... almost every city in the League would work to slap Chicago's ears down," he promised Harold Dailey in 1948. But expansion hadn't worked in 1944, and it didn't work in 1948, either. Crowds for games that featured the Colleens were noticeably smaller than usual, all around the circuit. Nor did the Sallies draw particularly well.

In 1948, the League would claim that overall attendance had reached one million, but even this was an exaggeration—the actual figure was 910,000. This was about 120,000 more than in 1947, but two-thirds of that increase was accounted for by home games in Springfield and Chicago. In other words, both expansion teams together added a mere 80,000 people all season long—a pitiful showing, especially considering the potential audience in a city the size of Chicago. Only half the other teams showed any increase in attendance at all. In Muskegon, where unemployment continued to rise because of postwar layoffs, 60,000 fewer people came out to the ballpark to see the Lassies play in 1949. Rockford, the play-off champions, ran an $11,000 deficit. The League grossed more money than ever before—which was fine for Meyerhoff, he got his cut—but several teams had peaked, for any number of reasons, and had nowhere to go but down. The League could make money by adding cities, or by extending both the regular season and the play-offs. But an individual club had to face the fact that an extended season would do it no good, that its dwindling audience would be spread too thin over too long a period of time.

Still, the clubs wanted to believe that solutions were possible. They sought a scapegoat and decided that poor financial management coupled with poor direction from Meyerhoff and Carey were the major culprits. The clubs' response was to tighten the League's belt. They cut expenses for administration, publicity and scouting. As of 1949, collective spring training was abolished. That decision had far-reaching consequences. Spring training—along with pre-season exhibition games—had provided the game with a sure-fire kickoff each season, attracted the national press and uncarthed at least some worthwhile talent.

Despite the belt-tightening, Meyerhoff and Carey found the resources to chase the dream of setting up other female leagues, both in the U.S. and elsewhere. Carey had begun trying to make this fantasy a reality in 1947, with spring training in Cuba. He and Meyerhoff planned a 1947 post-season mini-tour, involving an all-star team. It was to have played in Cuba, the Dominican Republic, Puerto Rico, Panama, Venezuela, Mexico and Texas. The players made it as far as Venezuela, but the tour ran out of steam early on when the Latin American promoters proved unreliable. One of the players, Mary Rountree, reported that "the people have loads of money; it flows like water." This welcome news compelled the League to press ahead. In February, several more players toured Cuba and Puerto Rico, to appear against local female teams.

The All-American hoped that these excursions could be parlayed into something called the International League of Girls Baseball, which would have played in Florida during

December, Venezuela during January, Puerto Rico during February and Cuba during March. But the players were just on loan to the Latin American organizers. The League had no responsibility except to insist on standards being maintained. When schedules failed to pan out or salaries were slow in coming, there was nothing that Carey or Meyerhoff could do.

In early 1949, the All-American continued to ship players abroad—this time to Nicaragua, Panama and Costa Rica. Once again, the Latin American promoters failed to provide the necessities of life (including some of the salaries owed), and Meyerhoff covered the shortfall from the League treasury. He also inaugurated a series of Players Development Tours, involving rookies and second-stringers, who wore the uniforms of the defunct Colleens and Sallies. These tours ranged over Arkansas, Oklahoma, Texas, Louisiana, Virginia and New Jersey. Periodically, the League would call on one of the teams for a replacement and a rookie would get a chance to move up to the All-American "majors."

Meyerhoff would have been better advised to keep an eye on matters close to home. The autumn of 1948 saw the departure of players such as Christine Jewett—not a star, but a solid performer, hard-working and popular with the crowds. The injured Pat Keagle wouldn't be coming back, nor would Dottie Collins. The 1948 switch to the overhand throw had sorted out those who couldn't or wouldn't adjust, and there were plenty of other reasons to say goodbye. Daisy Junor found that the years had caught up with her. She was about to turn twenty-nine and thought that it was the right moment to hang up her cleats. "I'd had about enough," she says. "I was always getting blisters on my heels, always getting fixed up in the dugout rather than running." Bonnie Baker, who was now past thirty, extended her career by switching positions, forsaking her catcher's mask for the slightly less punishing duties of a second baseman—but she, too, was buying time.

Others made a choice between marriage and career. Arleene Johnson played her last game in 1948. That winter, back in Saskatchewan, she had met a man she wanted to marry and she didn't think it appropriate for a wife to play ball. It was a dilemma that many players faced, although not all of them made the same decision as Johnson. Pepper Paire got engaged in mid-1948 and promised to marry her sweetheart when the season ended, but the chance of a tour in Latin America convinced her to break her promise. "He told me, 'If you go, that's it,'" she says. "So I said 'Adios,' and I went." A very few women married and kept on playing, but most would realize sooner or later that they couldn't mix the two careers.

Still others had begun to realize the financial costs of continuing to play pro ball. Every autumn they would return home or settle down in their team city to look for a winter job. If they were lucky, they had a steady job they could leave in the spring and pick up again at the end of the season. Several players entered college and studied all winter, financed by their baseball savings. But many All-Americans lived a fairly hand-to-mouth existence, making ends meet with low-paying temporary jobs.

As the League pursued its relentless cutbacks, salaries failed to keep pace with inflation. To a woman in her twenties, her playing days numbered, a steady job of any kind began to look attractive. No one could make long-term plans. Doris Satterfield, for example, didn't take up nursing until after she left the League, because no employer would hire a person who hit the road every time May rolled around. For the majority of players, staying in the All-American meant putting the rest of their lives on hold. This sacrifice would eventually become too great.

The winter of 1948 had marked a turning point for Betty Tucker. At the end of previous seasons, she'd gone back to Detroit just as her mother was returning to her job as a schoolteacher. Tucker had fallen into the easy role of unpaid housekeeper, and it made her lackadaisical about finding another job, especially the kind she might pick up for just a few months. "I can remember going shopping for groceries and looking at the girl behind the counter and thinking, 'Oh, my goodness, she stands there all day long for eight hours doing this.'" Against her mother's advice, and with $150 in her pocket, Tucker drove to California. "I thought I was rich with that kind of money in those days," she says, "but there was a recession that year and not much work." By the time she finally found a job as a cashier, she was down to her last quarter. She remembers rolling her car into a gas station and telling them to put in twenty-five cents' worth. When she had made it back to her rented room, the landlady told her there'd been a telegram. Alarmed, Tucker assumed there was bad news from Detroit and wondered how she'd get back home. But her mother was psychic, not ill: "She'd sent me a $20 money order, and I thought, 'How did she know?'" When she returned home, Tucker vowed she'd never be out of a job again—a decision that would cause the All-American League one or two headaches.

In 1949, the players assembled once more, training with their individual clubs. The League had shrunk to eight teams, grouped once again in a single division. And once again, in mid-season, there were more changes for players to grapple with. The ball was made even smaller and the pitcher's mound set back five feet. Pitchers who were still trying to adjust to throwing overhand were once more playing off-balance. The changes had the desired effect, though. The pace of the game was altered. There were more home runs, more .300 hitters. Late-inning rallies were possible, and fans once again stayed around until the last out.

Such changes made it even harder for rookies to get time on the field. The League had a solution; it introduced the highly contentious "Rookie Rule," which masqueraded as player development. Every team had to have a rookie—someone who'd played fewer than fifty games—in the lineup at all times. These players tended to get dumped into right field, a baseball diamond's least active corner. Even so, veterans felt that the rule blunted a novice player's edge. She got to play whether she deserved to or not. That, says Dorothy Ferguson, changed a player's attitude for the worse, and it showed when she made an error: "Rookies would be shown up in some way, and they'd be trying to hold back a grin. Old timers would never have done that. It was all business to them."

Finding new baseball talent was one of the responsibilities of Meyerhoff's Management Corporation. Its failure to do so, coupled with other League problems, began to make converts to Harold Dailey's position—that the League should buy Meyerhoff out. The clubs had been reluctant to come to that conclusion for a couple of reasons. Meyerhoff had done well when it came to generating publicity, and the club owners realized that they were ill-equipped to drum it up themselves. They concentrated on their towns; it made them think small, an attitude that had forced on Meyerhoff many of the actions they now blamed him for. Now, as gate receipts began to drop and clubs began to talk of folding, the question of where to find new franchises arose. That, too, would be Meyerhoff's task, and nobody else wanted to spend the time or energy to take it on. But if the clubs couldn't agree to be rid of Meyerhoff, they could do without Max Carey, whom they perceived as unduly free-spending.

The result was that Carey was replaced, in typical All-American fashion. In late 1949, while Carey was on vacation, the League executive replaced him with Fred Leo, the publicity director, also a Meyerhoff protégé but one who had proved his worth. Leo had come up through the ranks, in a manner of speaking, starting as a director of the Peoria Redwings club. He had proven himself capable and frugal, thus winning the owners' respect. But when Carey returned, Meyerhoff delayed telling him the bad news until a place could be found for him in the Chicago Cubs' organization. Dailey later wrote that Meyerhoff feared Carey would be offered a job by the Chicago League. As a result, Dailey wrote, waspishly, "Carey was back in his office and did not know that he was out and Fred Leo was in the office of President.... That is five weeks that the League is paying $1,100 [*sic*] a week and neither man able to work on account of the other being present. Carey $650 and Leo $550 a [month] salary and us broke as a league." Eventually the transition took place, and Carey stayed in the All-American. The following year he took over as manager of the Fort Wayne Daisies.

One of Leo's first challenges in his new post was to put the Chicago League in its place. All pretense of cooperation had by now collapsed and wholesale raiding was underway again. By this time, the standard All-American contract included an option on a player's services, meaning that she was bound to negotiate with the League before signing elsewhere. The option hadn't prevented several players from jumping to the Chicago League, if it was in their interest to do so. The deciding factor was usually money, although Audrey Wagner made the switch so that she could attend university rather than bounce around the countryside.

Most players waited until the season was over and jumped before their team had come to count on their services for the following spring. Not so Betty Tucker, whose California experience had convinced her to settle where she could get a year-round job. Tucker had returned to the League in 1949, joining the Kenosha Comets, then being managed by Johnny Gottselig. When the changes to the ball and diamond came in mid-season, the Comets—with Tucker part of their pitching staff—hit a prolonged losing streak. After a particularly awful series against Racine, Gottselig chewed them out. To flee his wrath, most of the team headed for a club, where they ate, drank and danced past curfew with a crew of sailors who providentially appeared. When they returned to their hotel, there in the lobby sat Gottselig and the chaperon. "So," says Tucker, "we lined up, put our hands on each other's shoulders and marched past them to the elevators and up to our rooms. Nobody said a thing."

The next night, at a pre-game meeting, Gottselig had plenty to say. He ripped into the team, accusing them of not caring whether they won or lost. Stung by his attack, the Comets won handily that night, with Tucker on the mound. But she couldn't shake Gottselig's criticisms. She resented the pressure and the mid-season changes to the game. Tucker decided to take Frank Darling up on his offer to jump. As he had urged many players to do in the past, she called him up, and the next day he arrived to drive her personally to Chicago.

This suited Tucker well. She could play a familiar sort of game (the Chicago League still played softball, with an underhand pitch) and get a steady day job, too. But none of this suited Fred Leo in the least. Fed up with Darling's poaching, especially in mid-season, Leo launched a flurry of lawsuits on behalf of the League, starting with Darling and the Chicago League, and winding up with Tucker, who was sued personally for $5,000. Tucker's mother read about it in the Detroit newspaper and called, fearful that her daughter might wind up in jail. Tucker was unconcerned: "I'm telling her, 'Look, I just decided to change leagues.' And she's saying, 'You can't do that, you signed a contract.' She was ready to put a lien on the house. I told her, 'I'm not worried about $5,000,' but she says, 'You're not, but I am.'"

In fact, the All-American didn't want Tucker's hide. It wanted to stop the raids—a determination strengthened by the news at the end of the 1949 season that Connie Wisniewski had been signed by Darling for 1950 for $250 a week. Tucker was a good pitcher, but Wisniewski was a star. Other big-name draws might decide to follow her.

Leo found he didn't have to follow through on the legal threats. The All-American found an ally, oddly enough, in the Chicago League's other team owners. By this time, they'd decided that they couldn't afford a salary war, even if Darling could. So it was that, by the time 1950 rolled around, a new agreement had been reached between the rival leagues, which found them recognizing suspensions and exchanging rosters well in advance. The All-American's suit against Tucker disappeared, and the League acknowledged Wisniewski's right to move to Chicago.

The Wisniewski episode, however, cut deep. Darling had lured her away to his club, the Music Maids, with promises of a salary the All-American couldn't hope to match. Many of the players recall being courted by Frank Darling, an official of the International Brotherhood of Electrical Workers for whom owning and managing a winning women's softball team had become a mania. He had decided to buy a championship team at any cost, and had offered Wisniewski—besides the $1,000 a month—a chauffeured limousine and a two-year contract stipulating that she'd be paid even if injured. The last condition had been demanded by Wisniewski, and when Darling consented, she had hopped. She could go back to being a pitching champ once again.

Wisniewski spent a season with the Maids, delivered to and from each game by Darling's bodyguard, who also began to take her out for dinner—not part of her contract. Wisniewski and the bodyguard even discussed marriage, but the ball player decided against it. "He lied to me," she says. "He had a daughter he didn't tell me about. He happened to be the same religious faith as I was, but he didn't tell me that, either. And he didn't appeal to me. The kind of man who went for me was two tons and six-foot-four. I wanted a man who was six-foot-four, all right, but I wanted a skinny man. I was gonna fatten him up."

Wisniewski found that Chicago wasn't to her liking. "In all the years I played with the All-American, I'd never had anyone approach me and say, 'I'll give you $500 or $1,000 if you throw tomorrow's game.' But it happened in Chicago. It got so that they'd start to make overtures, and I'd just walk away. I don't think it had anything to do with the Chicago League itself; it was just the gamblers." Chicago played rough, and the All-American didn't—it was as simple as that.

At the end of her first season with the Music Maids, Wisniewski decided to return to the All-American. The League had a rule blackballing players who'd left the League for Chicago, but the rule was relaxed for Wisniewski. Players of her caliber were too few and far between.

All in all, 1949 was not a good year for the All-American. Only two clubs showed a profit, and five registered losses ranging between $15,000 and $27,000. One broke even. Rockford had, predictably, won the championship, and cutbacks continued unabated. In 1950, umpires were no longer allowed to officiate outside their home cities, to save on traveling expenses. The League board members argued over whether or not players should take a salary cut. In fact, throughout this dismal period, some players were voluntarily going without pay for weeks at a time in order to keep their teams afloat. Meyerhoff pointed out that since members of the Players Development Teams were playing for $25 a week, regular players should make the sacrifice as well. Some board members argued that a cut would void everyone's contract, and that they should at least allow players to quit.

Finally, Dr. Dailey, his eye as always on the bottom line, proposed a compromise—eliminate meal money paid for on-the-road games. That decision started another brouhaha. When they heard the news, members of the South Bend Blue Sox walked out just before the 1950 play-offs. South Bend's management got them back by paying the meal money itself, on the grounds that other teams were doing the same in secret. But to no avail. Rockford won the championships again, losing, over the course of the year, some $3,000, in spite of a stringent budget, which prompted the club's president, Wilbur Johnson, to insist that Management Corporation cut its share of the gate in half. Meyerhoff reluctantly agreed, but club losses didn't stop.

In short, the 1950 season was a debacle. The Muskegon Lassies folded halfway through, and the team was relocated to Kalamazoo. This change brought one of the most interesting developments during the second half of the League's existence. When the Lassies were shifted to Kalamazoo, the League asked Bonnie Baker to be their manager. It was an unplanned mid-season move to fill the gap left by an unsatisfactory male manager who hadn't been able to carry through on his ambitious plans for the team. South Bend was in a quandary about whether or not to release Baker. On the one hand, Dailey thought of her as the "brains" of the Blue Sox team. But, on the other, he didn't want to lose the chance of being able to boast that it was South Bend that had given the League its first full-fledged woman manager. Baker went.

Baker did well, moving the club from its last-place standing to fourth. The local newspaper reported that she'd inherited "a floundering, colorless group, and turned it into a fighting, winning team. No one could do more." At this time, Baker was featured in a film produced by Grantland Rice, the dean of American sportswriters, titled *The Kalamazoo Clouters*. The League still viewed her as a public-relations asset. At season's end, Kalamazoo wanted her back, but the other club directors were against female managers on anything but an emergency basis. In the winter of 1950, they passed a resolution to that effect. Only once more before the League collapsed would a player be made manager—the following year Ernestine "Teeny" Petras took over as manager for a few weeks in Kenosha.

As usual, the explanations vary. Promoting a player who'd be capable of wearing the manager's hat meant taking a seasoned veteran off the field—a player with brains, experience and guile. Baker thinks that the League wanted to continue its policy of hiring well-known male baseballers: "They didn't want me beating former big-league stars." On the other hand, Carl Orwant, a member of the Grand Rapids board, suspected that money was the deciding factor: "They didn't want to take a $400-a-month player and make her into a $500-a-month manager."

Racine—a founding city—called it quits after the 1950 season, and the Belles moved to Battle Creek, Michigan. The trickle of departing players became a flood. The League's board admitted, in a confidential memo, that it was "woefully weak of capable talent." The Kenosha Comets and the Peoria Redwings folded in 1951. The single advantage was that their players could be apportioned out in what had become, by 1952, a six-team League.

Over the course of two seasons, the All-American lost something like two dozen experienced veterans, and many who replaced them weren't of the same quality. They couldn't have been; the veterans had been playing a game for years that was radically different from the softball that the rookies were used to playing. The rookies were still paid $55 a week—exactly the same as in 1943. Only four or five players per team made the $100 a week maximum. Raises were limited to $5 a week each year. Sometimes it materialized, sometimes it didn't. Wages were by now on par with minor-league ball—a poor inducement to sign your life away.

Meanwhile, the press had begun to place some of the blame for the League's troubles on the players. The Grand

Rapids newspaper stated that it was tired of "dismal and colorless" baseball, despite "all-out efforts on the part of club owners
and the league to make it better." The trouble, said the sports
editor, was that the players were blasé: "The girls have been too
long in the league, too satisfied with their jobs and taking
things far too much for granted. They know there is a scarcity
of good girl players and a manager can't get along without
them, no matter what they do or do not do." That wasn't fair to
players who had little control over how their clubs were being
managed, but the sense that the troubles were all their fault
began to grow.

Many anguished discussions took place, centering on the
need to recapture the public's affection. The directors could
see that television viewing, stiff competition from other, more
exciting, professional sports and a hundred other shifting reali-
ties of a postwar world had to be taken into account. Nevertheless, the issue they seized on harked back to the earliest days of
the League—femininity.

In one of Meyerhoff's exchanges with Wilbur Johnson, he
wrote that Wrigley had sold him the League on the understanding that he, Meyerhoff, would be a "watchdog" when it
came to proper standards. He confessed that he been "negli-
gent in this respect." Fred Leo was quick to take his cue. He
launched a series of closed-door meetings with chaperons,
managers and players themselves. (At this time, the League
proposed the idea of chaperon-players, purely as a cost-cutting
measure. About half a dozen women took on this double duty,
including the venerable Choo Choo Hickson. They even
experimented with doing away with chaperons, but that idea
didn't last more than half a season.)

The All-American's rules were rewritten. After establishing
a "balancing committee" to deal with such perennial sources
of tension and bad will as allocation, artificially prolonged
play-offs and mounting debt, the regulations got down to the

heart of the matter. A series of punishments was laid out for such infractions as on-field profanity, after-hours visits to bars and the still-prevalent habit of slugging umpires. Umpires, for their part, were given authority to prowl the stands prior to a game, in search of fraternizers. Most players, said Leo, were cooperative, but a few would "feel the sting of a shortened paycheck if they don't comply." The dress code was altered to ban "masculine hair styling, shoes, coats, shirts, socks and T-shirts" at all times, both on and off the field, and the curfew was tightened up.

So much for Meyerhoff's and Leo's paternalistic designs— but both of them were coming to the end of their League careers. In 1950, the clubs summoned up their resolve and decided to be rid of Management Corporation. Meyerhoff may have touched off this revolt himself when he once more publicly recommended that some teams move to larger, more hospitable centers. He pointed out that the touring teams— composed of $25-a-week rookies who weren't considered sufficiently skilled to make the League—were drawing crowds of 6,000-plus in New York and Washington, D.C. He ignored the likelihood that they were one-shot curiosities. Meyerhoff also said that civic ownership (the local boosters) wasn't working, that individual ownership (big-city, big-time entrepreneurs) was the wave of the future.

This was a slap in the face of the team owners, who had (for all their warts) borne with the League through good times and bad, loyal to its founding premise. Every spring, they had written the same welcoming speech for the mayor's delivery, planted the same hopeful stories (money had been found, fans had responded and the club would be solvent once again) in local newspapers. They had devoted years of their lives, and in many cases appreciable sums of money, to make the League a credit to their cities. Why had they continued? Dr. Dailey proposed a cynical explanation. "Perhaps it is as Ken Sells said," he wrote. "The short skirts and the girls do a lot of it." A more likely reason was that, once in, it was difficult to get out. Having attached their names and reputations to the League for so long, they didn't want to give up. The All-American was their link to the past—to old values, shared experience and common purpose, to the war, when people pulled together. Community ownership had defined the League from its outset. Now Meyerhoff was suggesting they sell out to the highest bidder, to men like Frank Darling.

It cost the clubs $8,000 to buy out Meyerhoff's interest in the All-American—and, in later years, he would admit that he'd done rather well. "The proof that it was a sound enterprise," he told a researcher, "is that I operated it for about six years or more and ended up with a very substantial profit."

Ironically, in the midst of all this change and dissension, some clubs began to do better than they ever had before—at least on the field. After eight years without a pennant, South Bend suddenly topped the standings in 1951 and won the championship, that year and the next. On the balance sheet, however, things continued downhill. At a board meeting in August, president Fred Leo reported that the League owed $6,600 and had $168 in the till. He then distributed copies of his resignation.

Leo was replaced by Harold Van Orman, a prominent hotel owner from Fort Wayne who had been a director of the Fort Wayne Daisies for many years. Like those before him, Van Orman had grand plans for reorganizing the League, including bringing it back to eight-team strength. He asked Chet Grant, sportswriter and former League manager, for his opinion. What he got was a diatribe against what Grant thought was the real problem—"indecorous femininity." Decorum was in decline, he said, and "had been progressively for several years." He pointed to the Racine Belles as "a horrible example of a situation where the girls run the show." Attendance had dropped even in the thick of the pennant race, he claimed, because of their hard-boiled ways, what he called a "depreciation in their reputation for decorous feminine deportment."

Grand Rapids and Rockford were on the skids as well, affected by the same "growing overall indifference of the league to the importance of sustaining the illusion [*sic*] that the girls are nice as well as skillful." Nor was Grant alone in finding fault with the players. A few months earlier, Dr. Dailey had noted that the South Bend players had met with the business manager to express a number of concerns. "They wanted to know why they had to have a play-off, how the club share was arrived at, and how the money was distributed to the players," he wrote. "They also wanted to know the finances of the clubs in the league, which was, and is, none of their business. It was the usual group of girls, and for my dough they can go straight to hell."

And so the League straggled on, locked in a losing battle. Attendance and revenues continued their downward slide. But somehow the clubs endured, sustained by never-say-die fans and players for whom the League continued to exert appeal. A new crop of rookies kept appearing, year by year. The post-1948 period had its own stars, who were as beloved by fans as those of glory days, and whose exploits are recalled just as warmly at their annual reunions. The League was still something to aim for, the top of the pole, the only game in town. But even those who dreamed of playing had realized the fragility of their ambition. Marilyn Jenkins, the Grand Rapids bat girl, remembers hoping that the League would last long enough for her to play. It did, and she became the Grand Rapids catcher until the League's demise.

Signs of decay were everywhere. Local newspaper coverage dwindled, a victim of decreasing fan interest and high costs. The sports editor was usually paid both by the newspaper to cover an event and by the League, as official scorer. Yet, though the papers paid for the telegraph costs, they often had difficulties getting the results for the morning paper of out-of-town games. The newspapers complained of paying too much for too little. The cash-strapped League agreed to changes in the scorekeeping that would have made the job of covering games easier and a little cheaper for the newspapers, but the League couldn't enforce them. Home-city reports in some papers became perfunctory.

The clubs, especially the new franchises, couldn't stabilize. Battle Creek, which had taken over the Belles in 1951, lasted only two seasons, and the team then moved to Muskegon, which must have been missing the departed Lassies. This period was ruled by the Fort Wayne Daisies, under the transplanted Bill Allington, who won the pennant in 1952 and 1953 but lost the play-offs both years, first to the Blue Sox and then to the Grand Rapids Chicks. By the end of 1953, total debt for all the clubs was a staggering $80,000. The League was ready to call it quits. President Van Orman made the announcement only to discover he was out of step. He received a "deluge" of protest calls. He convened a meeting at which the clubs' directors decided to give it one more try.

It seems miraculous that in 1954 the clubs could still find local backers for what seemed inevitable losses. Only one team—the Muskegon Belles—dropped out. That left Rockford, South Bend, Grand Rapids, Fort Wayne and Kalamazoo as the cities prepared to field teams. In April 1954, they announced their intention to continue, with reduced rosters (and, of course, reduced salaries).

In many respects, the League was scarcely recognizable. Players behaved more or less as they pleased, in and away from the park. Standards were lax for everybody. Sue "Sis" Waddell, who didn't join the League until 1951, remembers when she and some of her teammates went out joyriding in the middle of the night. They were picked up by the police for speeding and had to call their manager. At three o'clock in the morning, he didn't answer his phone and neither did the chaperon when she was called, prompting rumors that the two were together. For the players, there was no other fall-out. A few years before, it would have been grounds for sending players home.

Exhibition games against men's teams were commonplace. Rented buses were long gone, and the clubs gypsied around from town to town, packed in players' cars. Marilyn Jenkins realized that the All-American's days were numbered when her week's pay was counted out in one dollar bills. "It was the gate receipts from the night before," she says.

An advertisement for a double-header in South Bend sounded like a freak show. Still assuring people this was "real baseball ... not softball," it urged fans to come out and see the "Baseball Babes!" and the cow-milking contest that would be part of the entertainment.

Some of the early managers were still around. Bill Allington had declined to re-sign with the Rockford club in 1953 on the grounds that he planned to return to California to attend to business interests there. But just after the Peaches announced they had hired Johnny Rawlings, the Fort Wayne Daisies released the news that Allington was theirs. Both men were back for 1954. Besides the old rivals, Woody English, a former Chicago Cub, was piloting the Grand Rapids Chicks. Karl Winsch, married to South Bend's ace pitcher, Jean Faut, would manage the Blue Sox for the fourth year in a row, while Mitch Skupien headed the Kalamazoo Lassies.

Given the League's rocky reality, the general level of good cheer was surprising. South Bend went so far as to hire a full-time business manager from the Detroit Tigers, in hopes of balancing their books. By mid-season, rumors were finding their way into print that the clubs wanted to be rid of the latest League president (Earl McCammon, who in fact was now called the League's "commissioner"). This, they said, was because they needed an abler man to guide them into 1955. They also took the last step in converting to men's baseball. The League adopted the nine-inch regulation-size ball and expanded the basepaths to eighty-five feet—once again in mid-season. Advertising hyped the changes: "Home Runs and Power Plays! The most daring revision ever made in girls professional baseball! Can the girls handle this small ball? Come Out and See Tonight!" To complete the sense of déjà vu, they issued a string of statements to the effect that the League hoped to re-expand, this time to Chicago, where it held chummy discussions with a former owner in the now-defunct Chicago League.

By this time, only a handful of All-American veterans remained. Dorothy Ferguson Key was still with the Rockford Peaches. Gabby Ziegler remained with the Grand Rapids Chicks and Dorothy Schroeder with the Kalamazoo Lassies. Most of their former teammates were long gone, back to factories, farms and families.

Faced with collective adversity, the clubs had pledged to be more cooperative during the season, lending players whenever necessary to keep the teams evenly matched. By now, they had dispensed with the old allocation system.

The crowds weren't huge, but some franchises drew two thousand fans a night. The latest rule changes once again conspired to produce more hits and home runs. In fact, in Kalamazoo, which had the League's smallest playing field, the Lassies ordered up a special "deadened" ball that wasn't so easy to knock out of the park. All this resulted in a close race among the five teams that ended, in the closing days of August, with Allington's Fort Wayne Daisies in first place. Rawlings' Peaches, in fifth place, were eliminated from the play-offs.

This paved the way for a pair of best-of-three semi-finals. The second-place South Bend Blue Sox played the fourth-place Kalamazoo Lassies and came out on top, set to play the winners of the Fort Wayne-Grand Rapids series. That series packed considerably more punch.

Fort Wayne had now topped the standings three years straight, only to lose three play-off championships. The Daisies, led by Allington, wanted to win. However, events seemed to be conspiring against them. Back in the spring, to prove good faith in the new atmosphere of cooperation, South Bend had lent Fort Wayne its second-string catcher when the Daisies' first-stringer was injured. By the end of August, South Bend's catcher was herself immobilized. The Blue Sox asked for and received their second-stringer back, forcing the Daisies to make do with one of their pitchers behind the plate. This player had, in fact, caught for other teams, but Allington didn't want her for the play-offs. He wanted the League's top-ranked catcher, Ruth Richard, a Rockford Peach. Commissioner McCammon polled all the club presidents and everyone, including Roy Taylor of Grand Rapids, had approved. Unfortunately, Taylor, who was now sole owner of the Chicks, had not informed his team.

The final best-of-three contest between the Daisies and Chicks was slated to begin at South Field in Grand Rapids. This was good news for the Chicks, who tended to falter badly on the road. An initial victory would get them off on the right foot.

At the first game, on a Saturday night, the Chicks and manager Woody English arrived to find the Daisies preparing to put Ruth Richard behind home plate. Marilyn Jenkins, catching for the Chicks, thought that "it was like the Boston Red Sox in the World Series taking Joe DiMaggio and Mickey Mantle and Yogi Berra, and it wasn't fair." English made a formal pre-game protest, claiming that Richard, having played all season for a team that was out of the play-offs, was ineligible. Allington argued that he had the commissioner's backing, and that Richard should stay. At this point, the Chicks left their dugout and returned to the clubhouse. Faced with a stadium full of restless fans, League officials negotiated a compromise. The Chicks would play under protest, on the understanding that the issue would be resolved before the second game on Sunday. Thus assured, the agitated Chicks pulled off a triumphant 8-7 win over Allington and the Daisies, scoring the winning run in the ninth inning with two out and the bases loaded.

On Sunday night, the action shifted to Fort Wayne's Memorial Stadium. The Chicks arrived to find 1,600 fans in the bleachers and Richard suiting up. English ordered the Chicks off the field. He would have been wise to follow them, but he remained to argue with Allington at home plate. No one can remember who swung first, but there was certainly a fistfight, and the umpire and others had to separate the two managers. The umpires forfeited the game to Fort Wayne—not because of the brawl, but because the Chicks, at English's direction, had defaulted.

Who was behind these events depends on whom you listen to. Marilyn Jenkins lays some of the blame on Allington, who "had a lot of ways to win." Gabby Ziegler remembers how belligerently English reacted. "He got very bull-headed about Fort Wayne having this other catcher. He wasn't going to have it. So he pulled the team off the field." Ziegler wasn't as worked up about it as some of the players were. "We had won the last game against them, even with Richard as their catcher. What was the difference?" But you couldn't argue with English. "The whole thing was like a nightmare. You'd like to forget it but you can't." She thinks also that the episode left a bad taste in Allington's mouth, that he didn't want to win that way. Nonetheless, says Jenkins, "that's the way Grand Rapids ended, and that was the end of the League. We didn't like to talk about it, but the more we thought about it, I think we'd make the same decision today."

The next day, the Chicks went home, leaving English and other club officials to sort matters out with Commissioner

McCammon. English reminded the others that the teams played for a share of the gate during the play-offs, and that Richard's presence loaded the dice against them. It was bad sportsmanship, he said, to salt the Daisies with another team's top player. Taylor, the Grand Rapids owner, was faulted on two grounds—for failing to inform his team of what he'd agreed to, and for not insisting that they perform the job they'd come to do. Some people think English led the walkout; others criticize him for giving in to his players. Memories differ, and it was a long time ago.

Fort Wayne went on to play Kalamazoo in the finals—and lost, by the way, in a surprise upset. Once again, a low-ranking team had snatched the championship from the season's top-ranked club. Meanwhile, McCammon banished English from League management and fined him $35 for failing to field a team. He was fined another $15, as was Allington, for the fight. The players' money was held in escrow until further notice. Only the Grand Rapids officials escaped without censure. They "did everything they could to prevent this unhappy occur-rence," McCammon concluded, and "are to be commended for their efforts."

All in all, it was a nasty way to end the League.

When the All-American's players took to the field in 1943, they were fulfilling not a dream, but a fantasy. For a young woman in 1940s America, a professional sports career of any kind was not a likely prospect. There were—as there are today—female tennis players and golfers. But women's professional softball— let alone baseball—simply did not exist. Wrigley created it, then gave up on it before it could prove itself.

Nor did the All-American keep pace with the changes that ebbed and flowed around it. The players never unionized (although there were rumors of group action in South Bend, in the early years). Unlike the major leagues, the All-American never integrated. Two black players tried out with South Bend in 1951. Their arrival was met by—in the carefully chosen words of the keeper of the League minutes—"various views from different cities."

In the United States, 7,000 girls play little league ball, as opposed to more than 2,500,000 boys. They are effectively discouraged from joining the boys' teams. Like Pepper Paire, they take a lot of guff.

As for the players of the All-American League, those who survive are now in their sixties and seventies. Age has taken some of their fire and dash away. Some live in comfortable retirement. Others—perhaps because of their gypsy existence—are less fortunate, but they have few regrets.

Every other year, someone else discovers them, and a magazine article or ten-minute television feature wonders whatever happened to Bonnie Baker. Well, Bonnie Baker and all the rest of them have found each other again. They have formed the All-American Girls Professional Baseball League Players Association. As early as 1943, Philip Wrigley promised that photos of the players of the All-American would hang in the Baseball Hall of Fame in Cooperstown, next to those of the men who made pro baseball history. It never happened.

It wasn't until 1988, after many years of lobbying by the Association, and thirty-four years after the League folded, that the Baseball Hall of Fame finally recognized women's professional baseball. In November 1988, a permanent display was installed amidst much fanfare.

The Association holds annual reunions, at which they salute the empty chairs and sing the "Victory Song." They correspond through a newsletter in which they publish poems and report on what they're doing and who amongst them needs help or a friendly letter.

Once upon a time in the midwest, they did something no one else has done. They were just kids, having fun and enjoying one another. They weren't thinking about being pioneers, about making history. They didn't realize what pioneers they were. Today, they look forward to the next reunion, living very much in the present but looking back on occasion through the glow of nostalgia to the best years of their lives, when they were young and strong and together, playing the game they loved and at which they excelled, with all the time in the world stretching out before them.

WHERE ARE THEY NOW?

It's been nearly forty years since the players of the All-American Girls Professional Baseball League filled their hometown diamonds. Forty years since the last time the local newspaper carried the box scores, since fans strolled along shady streets to the park to watch the Peaches or the Daisies or the Blue Sox play.

There were some who just wouldn't believe it was gone. After the 1954 season, a couple of dozen players joined together with Bill Allington as the Allington All-Americans and continued to tour the midwest for three seasons, playing games against men's and women's teams. When the contest was against men, they switched the batteries (the male pitcher and catcher playing for the women's team, and vice versa) to give the crowd a good show. They covered a lot of ground, from Ohio to the Dakotas. The players rode a bus that had seen better days, used friendly townspeople's basements as dressing rooms and camped out in cheap motels. They played rodeos and circuses; it was one step up from the days of the wandering Bloomer Girls.

"They were the best years of my life." It's the way most former players sum up their careers in professional baseball.

Some players married and raised families; others went back to school. The money they saved from playing baseball often financed the changes in their lives. Their years in the League gave most of the players confidence and a vision of a life outside the little town or city they'd grown up in. Many couldn't go back to fulfilling the ideal of the dependent, housebound wife and chose careers instead. Others would still have married if they could, but marriage on their terms didn't happen.

Many of the players settled in the towns they had played in and are still there today, still occasionally recognized by fans of the 1940s and '50s. Friendships couldn't be as easily dissolved as the League. Friendships that began on a baseball field in the midwest have continued all their lives. There are pockets of former players all over North America—Saskatchewan, California, Arizona, Florida, the eastern seaboard and the four midwestern states that were their stamping grounds.

In Grand Rapids, Dottie Hunter took up her off-season job—sales clerk in a jewelry store—full-time. Players couldn't break old habits. Former Chicks like Marilyn Jenkins and Earlene "Beans" Risinger still dropped by to let her know what they were up to and ask her advice about their education or their careers.

Some continued to play ball, although that meant returning to amateur softball. There were others who found softball too tame after the faster pace of professional baseball, and they opted to take up other sports.

For most of the players, life after professional baseball had its ups and downs. For a few, life has been hard, even tragic. Of those, perhaps the most tragic was Merle "Pat" Keagle. Although Keagle had retired from the League, girls' professional baseball was still a reality when "the Blonde Bombshell" of Grand Rapids was hit by cancer; she died before she was out of her thirties.

Most of the men connected with the All-American League— its managers, club owners and executives—are now gone. The exceptions are Ken Sells, the first League president, who retired to Phoenix, Arizona; Fred Leo, another League president, who lives in Colorado; and Harold Greiner, former Daisies manager, who is still in Fort Wayne, nearly blind, but surrounded by photos of his family and his "girls," those he coached and managed in the heyday of softball and women's professional baseball. Many of those women he coached still visit him from time to time.

Lou Arnold, South Bend Blue Sox pitcher, took a job with Bendix Aviation in South Bend and worked there for many years. "I made a good living," she says. "I have a good retirement. I met all these good people. I've had a wonderful life, and a lot of it is because I played ball right here."

Mary "Bonnie" Baker lives in Regina, Saskatchewan, where she returned after her stint as Kalamazoo manager. Bonnie was one of those who found that she couldn't return to softball after the League, although she tried. When she first returned home, Baker joined a team that was playing Class A softball. They went to the national championships in Toronto in 1953. "But after that it was downhill all the way," she says, and Baker put softball and baseball behind her for good.

Husband Maury died just a few years after she left the League. With a nine-year-old daughter to support, Mary returned to work full-time, as western Canada's first radio sports news director. Later she started work in a curling rink. She eventually became its manager and remained there until her retirement.

Arnold Bauer, now a widower, still lives in South Bend. He keeps in touch with former Blue Sox by telephone and mail.

Marge Callaghan (Maxwell) is in Vancouver, British Columbia. Her sister Helen Callaghan (St. Aubin) lives in Lompoc, California. Kelly Candaele, one of Helen's sons, helped to spark renewed interest in the League during the 1980s when he co-produced a half-hour video documentary on the All-American that has been shown on national public television.

Faye Dancer left the League after 1950, at the age of twenty-five, the victim of a herniated disk aggravated by her baseball career. She trained in electronics and also ran her own business for a few years, all in Santa Monica, California, where she still works and sees old friends. She and Pepper Paire and other former League players recently played parts in a television situation comedy about former ball players holding a reunion.

Judy Dusanko moved to Saskatchewan with her husband when she left the All-American. She took up amateur softball once again and her team won the western Canadian championships. Basketball was the sport she pursued during the winter. Eventually, she and her husband escaped the Canadian winters by moving to Arizona, where they live today.

Thelma "Tiby" Eisen worked in California's telecommunications industry for over thirty years. She was fortunate enough to join a growing company and became one of the first women to work with its installation crews. She invested in the firm and now lives in Palm Desert, California.

Dorothy Ferguson (Key) and her husband Don remained in Rockford, and they still live in the first house they bought after their marriage. They have grandchildren, and they continue to operate a home maintenance business. "Dottie" also helps out at the Dixie Cream Donut Shop, where fans periodically drop by to recall old times.

Dorothy "Snooky" Harrell (Doyle) played her last game in the League in 1952 and then went to Phoenix to play softball. Inspired by other players who decided to attend college, she became a physical education instructor. She owns a house in Los Angeles County, paid for by her baseball earnings, but she lives in Cathedral City, California, next door to Dorothy Kamenshek.

Irene "Choo Choo" Hickson still lives in Racine, home of the Belles. She remained with the Racine team until it folded in 1950 and then ran a restaurant called the Home Plate, for a number of years.

Chaperon Dorothy Hunter stayed in Grand Rapids, Michigan—the city that had been her home for ten years—after the League folded. She and her Chicks have been friends ever since. At one point, Hunter returned to her home town of Winnipeg, but there wasn't enough of her former life to keep her there. At the urging of her friends from the League, Hunter has resettled in Grand Rapids, and her Chicks, she says today, "look after me like I was their grandmother."

Lillian Jackson lives in Arizona. She played with the Parischy Bloomer Girls, a Chicago League team, for four years after she left the All-American, and worked full-time. She took up swimming as well as golf, and still plays the game in Arizona.

Marilyn Jenkins, first the Grand Rapids bat girl and later their catcher, is still in her home town. After her baseball career ended, Jenkins became an estate agent and built up a business for herself. She recently unearthed a large cache of old photos about the League in the estate of a local businessman. The photos have been donated to the League's archives in South Bend.

Christine Jewett (Beckett) has retired, with her husband, to the tiny Saskatchewan community of Stewart Valley. Like the other Saskatchewan players, she looks forward to reunions and keeps in touch with her former teammates.

Betsy Jochum quit the League in 1948 when they attempted to trade her away from South Bend. Using her earnings, she returned to Cincinnati to get a college education and became a physical education teacher until her retirement.

Arleene Johnson (Noga) returned to Regina, Saskatchewan, after the 1948 season and married. Johnson returned to curling and still plays. She lives with her second husband, not far from several children and grandchildren. She has been active in setting up an All-American exhibit in the Saskatchewan Sports Hall of Fame, which recently inducted all players from the province who played in the League.

Daisy Junor and her husband Dave are retired now. They spend winters in Arizona but return to Saskatchewan each spring.

Dorothy Kamenshek, slowed down by a back injury, quit the League in 1951 to go to Marquette University. She studied to be a physical therapist and eventually pursued a career in health administration. She lives in Cathedral City, California, and she and ex-teammate Snooky Doyle regularly take a run out to Palm Desert to visit Tiby Eisen.

Sophie Kurys played softball in Chicago and Phoenix for a few years after she left the League in 1950. Eventually she went into business in Racine, and lived there until 1972 when she moved to Phoenix, Arizona. Kurys continued working for a time; now she is retired. She golfs with neighbor Joanne Winter and with Nicky Fox and goes to all the reunions.

Millie Lundahl, the Peaches' chaperon, is still in Rockford, Illinois, busier than ever.

Elizabeth "Lib" Mahon, who had teaching credentials when recruited from her South Carolina home, went back to South Bend after she retired from the game. It was intended as a stop-gap measure, but she remained until her retirement. Mahon, Arnold and Jochum regularly get together, visiting each other's homes, and help keep the League archives in good shape.

Helen "Nicky" Nicol (Fox) didn't return to her home province of Alberta after she quit the League in 1953. She settled in Racine and later moved to Phoenix, Arizona, where she works at a local golf course and regularly meets for a game with other former League players.

Lavonne "Pepper" Paire (Davis) played amateur softball and bowled in California after she left the League in 1953. She also worked at Hughes Aircraft and raised three children. In 1963, Paire suffered a serious injury to her back when she had a disastrous fall. Slowed, but undaunted, she lives today in Van

Nuys, California. Paire has acted as consultant on the 1992 movie about the All-American, *A League of Their Own.*

Mary Rountree left the League in 1952 to go to medical school. She became a doctor, eventually specializing in anesthesia. She settled in Coral Gables, Florida, where she still lives.

Doris Satterfield has always been "grateful for the opportunity to get out of a small town and come here and live a life that made me very happy." After she left the League, Satterfield went back to nursing. She now lives, retired, on the outskirts of Grand Rapids, Michigan.

Dorothy Schroeder lives in Urbana-Champaigne, Illinois, with her twin brother. She still works, and she recently moved into a new house that they had designed and built.

Betty Tucker spent five years in the Chicago League after her contentious departure from the All-American. She also went back to school, and then worked in a manufacturing plant for sixteen years. During her spare time she took up golf and bowling, but she expanded her activities when she moved to Tucson, Arizona, to get away from the snow. Today she hikes, camps and travels whenever she can.

Joanne Winter left the League in 1950 when the Racine Belles folded, spent a year with the Chicago League, then became a professional golfer. She recently finished writing her memoirs and lives in Phoenix, next door to ex-Belle Sophie Kurys.

Connie Wisniewski retired from the League after the 1952 season because "I'd got a good job at General Motors and I didn't want to give it up." She played softball with the company team for a couple of years, although they wouldn't let her pitch, "because I had been a professional. You know, just to be fair to the other players." After twenty-eight years, in which she had worked her way up to inspector, Wisniewski retired to St. Petersburg, Florida, where she golfs, visits friends and goes to all the League reunions.

Alma "Gabby" Ziegler returned to Los Angeles and became a court reporter, eventually working for the Superior Court of Los Angeles County. For her, "softball can't hold a candle to baseball," and so she never played again, although she did umpire some games. Golf became the important sport in her life, and it still is. She lives now in San Luis Obispo, California, where she "golfs, delivers Meals on Wheels and socializes."

ALL-AMERICAN GIRLS PROFESSIONAL BASEBALL LEAGUE, 1943-1954

Kenosha Comets	1943-51	Kenosha, Wisconsin
Racine Belles	1943-50	Racine, Wisconsin
Rockford Peaches	1943-54	Rockford, Illinois
South Bend Blue Sox	1943-54	South Bend, Indiana
Milwaukee Chicks	1944	Milwaukee, Wisconsin
Minneapolis Millerettes	1944	Minneapolis, Minnesota
Fort Wayne Daisies	1945-54	Fort Wayne, Indiana
Grand Rapids Chicks	1945-54	Grand Rapids, Michigan
Muskegon Lassies	1946-50	Muskegon, Michigan
Peoria Redwings	1946-51	Peoria, Illinois
Chicago Colleens	1948	Chicago, Illinois
Springfield Sallies	1948	Springfield, Illinois
Battle Creek Belles	1951-52	Battle Creek, Michigan
Kalamazoo Lassies	1950-54	Kalamazoo, Michigan
Muskegon Belles	1953	Muskegon, Michigan

AAGPBL CHAMPIONS

The League champion or pennant winner was the team that topped the standings at the end of the regular season. The play-off champion was the team that won the post-season play-offs.

	LEAGUE CHAMPIONS	PLAY-OFF CHAMPIONS
1943	Racine Belles (First half) Kenosha Comets (Second half)	Racine Belles
1944	Kenosha Comets (First half) Milwaukcc Chicks (Second half)	Milwaukee Chicks
1945	Rockford Peaches	Rockford Peaches
1946	Racine Belles	Racine Belles
1947	Muskegon Lassies	Grand Rapids Chicks
1948	Grand Rapids Chicks (Eastern Division) Racine Belles (Western Division)	Rockford Peaches
1949	Rockford Peaches	Rockford Peaches
1950	Rockford Peaches	Rockford Peaches
1951	South Bend Blue Sox	South Bend Blue Sox
1952	Fort Wayne Daisies	South Bend Blue Sox
1953	Fort Wayne Daisies	Grand Rapids Chicks
1954	Fort Wayne Daisies	Kalamazoo Lassies

AAGPBL BATTING CHAMPIONS

1943	Gladys "Terrie" Davis	.332
1944	Betsy Jochum	.296
1945	Mary Crews	.319
	Helen Callaghan	.299
1946	Dorothy Kamenshek	.316
1947	Dorothy Kamenshek	.306
1948	Audrey Wagner	.312
1949	Jean Faut	.291
	Doris Sams	.279
1950	Betty Foss	.346
1951	Betty Foss	.368
1952	Joanne Weaver	.344
1953	Joanne Weaver	.346
1954	Joanne Weaver	.429

INDEX

A

Ainsmith, Eddie, 133
All-American Girls Ball League, 58
All-American Girls Professional
Baseball League, 194, 196
All-American Girls Softball
League, 35
Allington, Bill, 52-53, 73, 77-81, 86-
87, 89-90, 107, 114-115, 120, 122-
125, 132-133, 140, 147-148, 150,
164, 166-167, 170, 188-193, 196
Anderson, Marie "Teddy", 65, 67
Armstrong, Charlotte, 31-32
Arnold, Lou, 94-95, 101, 118, 164,
198, 201
Avery, Fred, 88

B

Baker, Mary "Bonnie", 5, 33-35, 37-39,
43-45, 64, 74-75, 97, 108-109, 111,
116, 118-119, 122, 140, 159-160,
163-164, 174, 182-183, 194, 198

Baker, Maury, 37-38
Bancroft, Dave, 72, 147-148, 151
Bass, Dick, 168-170
Bauer, Arnold "Arnie", 95, 198
Bauer, Nadine, 95
Beirn, Ken, 11-12
Beyer Stadium, 170
Billings, Josh, 28, 73
Bishop, Hub, 34-35
Borchert Stadium, 59
Briggs, Rita "Junior", 148, 152
Briggs, Wilma, 150
Burmeister, Eileen, 49

C

Callaghan, Helen, 168, 198
Callaghan, Marge, 168, 198
Carey, Max, 58-59, 72, 74-75, 80-
84, 86-88, 95, 106-107, 111,
114-115, 125, 127, 129, 138-
139, 142, 151-153, 158-161,
166, 173-174, 177-178
Cartwright, Alexander, 14
Castro, Fidel, 127

ABOUT THE AUTHOR

Lois Browne discovered the story of the All-American League while working as a researcher for *W5*, CTV's investigative news program. Lois is a Toronto writer and editor. This is her first book.